GHOSTS OF
KEY WEST

DAVID L. SLOAN

Phantom Press
P.O. Box 4766
Key West, FL 33041

First Printing October 1998
Second Printing October 1999
10 9 8 7 6 5 4 3 2
ISBN 0-9674498-0-4

GHOSTS OF KEY WEST

DAVID L. SLOAN

Happy Hauntings!

KEY WEST

PHANTOM PRESS
KEY WEST, FLORIDA

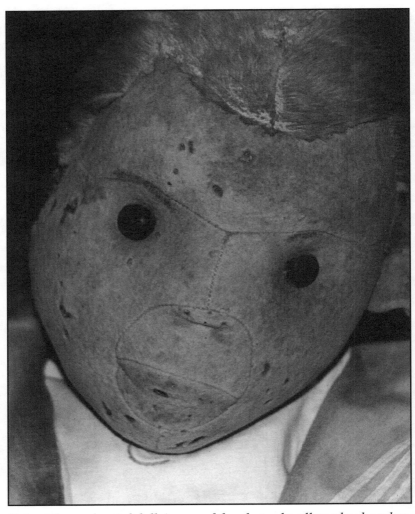

Robert the enchanted doll, in one of the photos he allowed to be taken.
Photo: David Sloan

To my three skeptics,
Cindy, Vladimir and Dr. Jeckyl

In loving memory of Victor & Mr. Hyde

The Key West Cemetary.

Photo: Rob O'Neal

CONTENTS

ACKNOWLEDGEMENTS

Special thanks to everyone who made this book possible. My family and friends for their support and encouragement; Mickey Melchiondo and Aaron Freeman for their inspiration; Dave Lapham, author of *Ghosts of St. Augustine*; and Tom and Lynda Hambright of the Monroe County Public Library.

My eternal gratitude to everyone from the haunted locations throughout Key West for taking the time to share your experiences. Your assistance in gathering this information is invaluable.

In researching "For Better or For Worse," I referred often to *Undying Love* by Ben Harrison. Though this story has been told a hundred times over, no one has managed to capture the feeling of this bizarre tale the way Ben has.

PREFACE

The hardest part about writing a book on the ghosts of Key West was deciding which stories to use. In the years since I started the Ghost Tours I have heard hundreds of stories from people who have experienced the supernatural, as well as having more than my fair share of personal encounters. Each story has an excitement and feeling of its own that words often can not express.

Some people believe in ghosts, others do not. My goal with this book is not to convert or change your beliefs in any way, but simply to provide you with some very unique stories from a very unique place. Whenever you want to escape to Key West, this book is there for you.

All of the names have been changed as a courtesy to the individuals involved, and in portions of the book dialogue has been added and composites used to better convey the events described.

I hope you enjoy reading these stories as much as I enjoyed writing them. The ghosts create a magic that makes Key West a place like no other.

The Ghosts of Key West

A horse-drawn funeral procession prepares to depart from the under-taker's on Bahama Street.

Photo: courtesy of Monroe County Public Library

When Key West is mentioned, many images come to mind. Some people are taken back to the days of the pirates and rumrunners when the island was little more than a convenient hideaway, while others are reminded of the warm waters and tropical palms just steps away from the hustle and bustle of Duval Street. In between there are the cigar makers, the spongers, the fishermen, artists, writers, and poets. Thousands of people chose Key West because it had that certain something which makes it a place like no other.

Some people call it magic, while others are left speechless because no words are appropriate to describe the feeling. Some people spend a great amount of time talking about it, while others just accept it and enjoy the experience on their own. Those searching for answers will often ask the question, "why Key West?" Part of the answer can be found in our name.

The first inhabitants of the Florida Keys were the Seminole and the Calusa Indians. Mainly inhabiting the Upper Keys, the peaceful Calusas were under constant threat of attack by the more aggressive Seminoles.

As the threat increased the Calusas began heading south, jumping from key to key hoping to avoid battle; and when they reached our southernmost island there was nowhere else to go. As a last alternative, the Calusas stood their ground. A bloody battle ensued and the few Calusa who survived are said to have paddled 90 miles to Cuba in their canoes to escape.

Things were quiet on the island until the 16th century when Spanish explorers arrived looking for safe trade routes through the straits of Florida. When they came ashore they found the beaches littered with bones from the bloody battle and describing what they saw in their native tongue, named the island "Cayo Hueso," Spanish for "island of bones."

Because many of the bones were found in trees or arranged in intricate patterns, there is speculation that the island was used as a massive burial ground.

Whichever the case, Cayo Hueso was corrupted changing "Cayo" to "Key" and "Hueso" to "West." Though later attempts were made to change the name to Thompson's Island and Allentown, mappers could not keep up with the changes and Key West stuck.

As with the name, the spirits remain. Ghosts of indians, pirates, wreckers, cigar makers, fishermen, artists and poets continue to be seen around town. Some say they are lost souls searching for the light, while others speculate that they are mere images trapped in time. I like to think that they are the ones who experienced that certain something in Key West and decided to stick around and enjoy the magic for just a little bit longer.

The Enchanted Doll

As Anne climbed the staircase to see how his work was coming, Gene assured her that he was not playing with dolls. "The kids say they saw him moving," she teased. "Maybe he did," Gene replied. "Maybe he did." A strange feeling came across the room and the doll seemed to glare at her. "We've got to get rid of that thing," she thought.

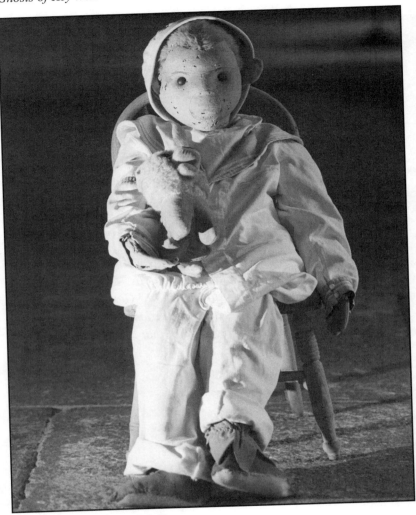

Robert, the enchanted doll.

Photo: Rob O'Neal

Anne Otto sat on the bench in front of her baby grand piano. From her posture alone it was easy to tell that she was a proud woman and the ease with which her fingers glided across the key board was a sure sign of a classically trained pianist. If it were not for her occasional breaks where she strove to make her timing exact, anyone passing by would be convinced that the beautiful music inside the most unique house on Eaton Street was coming from a recording.

Anne was always happiest at her piano. She had plans to tour the world as a concert pianist, but all of that changed after she met Gene. How romantic it was. He was an artist, she a musician; two Americans whose paths and whose hearts crossed in Paris. "It was probably that first portrait he painted of me," she thought to herself as her fingers continued to grace the keys. "What a charming young man he was back then."

"We have to be at the gallery in half an hour." Anne snapped back to reality as Gene's voice boomed from upstairs. It was to be a big show for Gene, but then again, every show was a big one to him. Anne was tired of all the fake smiles and empty compliments. She wanted to stay home and play her piano. Gene would have none of it.

Gene Otto was a unique character. He was born into a family of doctors but rejected medicine to pursue his love of art. His talent was second to none in Key West–and though he loved Anne even more than the paintings he so treasured, tonight's show was important to him and she should be more understanding. Did she not realize that he did all of this for her?

"You go without me," Anne said coldly, standing her ground. They had been through this before and she had always given in. "This time will be different," she told herself. Gene was not pleased with her unwillingness to go and an argument ensued. As words were exchanged, Anne rose from the piano and stormed through the kitchen to the back gardens. Gene followed, but as she began to raise her voice he backed down immediately. "Not outside. Do you want the neighbors to hear?" The argument was over. Anne went to her bedroom; Gene to his…and they prepared to go to the gallery.

It seemed pointless to argue with Gene. Blame was something he did not accept very well, especially when it came to his treatment of Anne. She knew he was an artist with an eccentric side to him. However, when it came to blaming things on Robert she knew that something strange was happening, but what could she do?

Robert was a doll. He was given as a gift to Gene Otto back in 1904 when Gene was only four years old. Some people say that it was a gift from his grandfather, but most agree that it came from a black girl, probably of Bahamian descent, who an acquaintance of the Otto family.

Gene and Robert had a strange relationship from the start. Gene's first gesture of friendship to the doll was to give him his name. It was at this point in his life that Robert Eugene Otto started going by "Gene." "Robert" seemed only too fitting for the doll, as it was crafted in young Gene's image. Constructed of cloth and stuffed with straw, Robert stood three feet tall, had dull black buttons for eyes and a face with monkey-like features. Over the years the doll took on the likeness of a burn victim.

Boy and doll spent all of their time together, and as in adulthood, whenever Gene was blamed for doing something wrong he refused to accept responsibility. "I didn't do it…Robert did it!" A pattern was developing that would haunt people for years to come.

Anne first discovered Robert when she and Gene returned from Paris. As a wedding gift they were to move into the house where Gene had grown up, and though Anne was a bit leery at first, all apprehensions disappeared when they pulled up in front of her new home.

It was in the heart of old town Key West just blocks away from everything. As Anne admired the Victorian architecture, complete with a royal turret rising majestically above the second floor, Gene explained that ship builders were responsible for the construction of their home which had been built around 1890. Anne felt like a princess in a fairy tale as she passed through the wrought iron gate with sculpted concrete pedestals and up the stairs towards the etched glass design of the entry way.

The inside of the house was equally impressive: polished hard wood floors; twelve foot ceilings; textured wallpaper. Everything was perfect. This would be an ideal home.

Shortly after moving in, Gene began spending a lot of time in the attic. When asked what he was doing, Gene replied that he was building a room for Robert. "Who is Robert?" Anne asked, unaware that they were expecting house guests. When Gene introduced her to the doll it was all she could do to keep from laughing. Was he really building this room for a doll? Gene did not think it was funny.

Construction in the attic was completed and Robert was the proud occupant of an 8x12 room complete with slanted ceilings, making it difficult for an adult to stand up. Though the attic itself was much larger, Gene thought this size would be best for Robert; and to ensure his comfort Gene furnished the room with scale-sized furniture and provided Robert with a wardrobe of clothing much like the ones he had worn as a child. Anne learned to tolerate this, but Robert was not limited to his room alone.

"You boys run along!" Anne scolded from her front porch at the small group of school kids looking mischievously at the top of her house. They did not seem to need much encouragement as they turned the corner and ran. "It moved, it moved!" she heard one of the kids saying. Curious as to what mischief they were causing, Anne stepped into the street and looked back at her house. "That damn doll." Gene had Robert perched in the window of the turret room looking out towards the street.

"Playing dolls with the school kids are you?" Anne joked to Gene, calling from his bedroom below. The only time she went to the turret room was to pose for the portraits that Gene painted of her. Not only was the sunlight in the turret ideal for painting, but it gave a grand view of the whole of Eaton Street. Anne was always excited to have company and she would sometimes watch for their arrival from the turret.

As Anne climbed the stairs to see how his work was coming,

Gene assured her that he was not playing with dolls. "The kids say they saw him moving." she teased. "Maybe he did," Gene responded. "Maybe he did." A strange feeling came across the room and the doll seemed to glare at her. "We've got to get rid of that thing," she thought.

July 25, 1974 was a sad day on the island. Anne Otto lost her husband and Key West lost a great artist. Gene had grown ill in his final years and it had taken its toll on Anne. Rumors around town said that Gene had become physically abusive to her in the months before his death, some saying he went so far as to lock her in a small closet. But those who knew the Ottos dismissed this as "pure rubbish." Some stories claimed that when Gene was confronted with the abuse he blamed the doll…

Shortly after Gene's death, Anne left Key West and headed for Boston to be with her family. Not wanting anything to do with the doll she had grown to hate, she left Robert behind in the attic room where he was encountered by many over the next two years. It is believed that a clause was included in the house's lease agreement specifying that Robert must remain the sole occupant of the attic room. This was the case until Anne's death in 1976. Yet strange stories started circulating as soon as she left the house.

"I was doing some work in the larger part of the attic of the house," a local plumber explained. "The people there wanted to make it an additional room so I was running the lines for a new toilet. The doll looked pretty creepy sitting there on the little chair holding its stuffed animal, but I had work to do so I didn't think much about it at first."

"As my work continued I had to make a few trips downstairs to get some parts from the van. Each time I returned I could swear the doll had moved a little bit. Like I said, I had work to do so I ignored it as much as I could, but when I'd finished the job and started descending the stairs I heard a little kid giggling behind me. When I turned around, the doll was on the opposite side of the room.

"The first thing I did was look to see where the kid was, but no one was there. I wasn't really frightened, but it was so weird that I just continued downstairs and left. Some of my tools are probably still up there."

Two men who rented the house in the mid 1970's share similar reports.

"There was constant noise coming from the room. Sometimes it was like little kids laughing and other times like someone was rummaging around. When it first started happening we would go upstairs to check it out, but always found nothing. It was only after a half dozen times that we realized the doll had moved. At first we blamed each other and laughed it off as a practical joke. Sometimes the doll's head would be looking in a different direction, other times its arms were propped up around the chair, and once its legs were even crossed. It started happening with greater frequency and we realized this was no joke; so we packed the doll away in a sea chest and never had any more problems with him. A few months later the owner of the house died. The building was sold and converted into a bed and breakfast."

The Artist House was a fitting name for Key West's newest guest house. A tribute to Gene Otto and all of Key West's artists, the building captured the feeling of the island like no other with its unique turret and freshly painted purple shutters. Over the years the house changed hands a few times, and Robert eventually found himself in a new home.

Von Phister Street was a nice place for Robert, but he missed the house he had grown up in. Sitting on the front porch all day watching the traffic go by helped to pass the time; and he certainly enjoyed resting up against the tree each Christmas. But he was old and fragile, so his owners took him to the East Martello Museum where he could be properly cared for. Upon arrival Robert was taken to a back room where he was eventually locked up and left covered with a bed sheet.

"Robert, you have a visitor," the young lady soothed as she carried the doll from his closet to a large oak table. "This man wants to take some photographs." She continued to pamper the doll, straightening the collar of his sailor suit, adjusting his sailor's cap, and pointing his pixie-shoed feet in the proper direction. Time had taken its toll on the doll, deteriorating the fabric on his face and exposing his straw and metal frame. The white of his costume was yellowed. Somewhere along the way he had even lost an ear, but that did not stop Eileene from speaking to him.

"Do you always talk to the doll like that?" David asked.

"Just to play it safe," she responded. With that, Eileene left and David began snapping photos.

A strange air filled the room. David was surrounded by a circle of dry heat and was overcome with the feeling of being watched. He turned around to see if Eileene was still in the room, but she was gone. Half a roll of film was shot from every angle possible, and then David moved in for some close-ups. The first two shots went fine, but Robert's hat was blocking his eyes. As David reached for the cap to remove it, Robert glared at him as if warning him to stop. The doll's pupilless eyes took on a life of their own and Robert actually looked as though he were about to move. "I've been reading too many stories," the photographer convinced himself.

He steadied the shot for a close up of the eyes and clicked the shutter. Nothing happened. He tried again and then checked over the camera in an attempt to detect the problem. Everything appeared to be in order so a third attempt was made. Nothing again. Deciding to call it a day, David placed his camera on the table. Three quick flashes went off and Robert looked as though he was laughing. David looked again at the dull black eyes and the energy seemed to fade away from the doll. "Definitely time to call it a day," David thought.

As word about the haunted doll continued to spread around town, more and more people came to visit Robert. Eventually the museum decided it would be easiest to put him in a display case; and he now sits locked behind glass with some other dark reminders of Key West's past. Reports of movement behind the glass as well as unexplainable camera malfunctions continue to this day. Jack Wharton tells his story:

"My friend and I heard about the doll and I was fascinated. I've had personal experiences with ghosts in the past so I was anxious to go to the museum but Frank was a complete skeptic. For the entire ride over, he kept repeating how silly this was. When the trolley stopped in front of the museum, we headed in and went straight to see Robert. I wanted to take some photos–Frank wanted to joke around.

"Hey big ear, is that your girlfriend in the case next to you? Frank taunted, referring to another stuffed doll nearby. I told him to stop messing around, but his taunting continued. I tried to snap a photo of Robert but my camera didn't work. Though I had just replaced the battery before coming to Key West, the red light indicated it was dead. Frank had a few pictures left on his roll so he volunteered to take some shots for me.

As the flash went off a strange sound came from Frank's camera. The film had jammed and his entire roll of Key West photos was destroyed in the process of unjamming it. No sooner had this happened than my camera started working again. Frank blamed it all on dumb luck, but I think it was Robert."

Though Robert no longer lives in the Artist House, the place is still bustling with activity. Strange things happen both inside and outside the house, but all of the activity is not to be attributed to Robert. He is joined by other spirits in the house.

Guests have reported doors opening and closing on their own. Lights turn on or off for no apparent reason, sometimes illuminating despite the fact that they are unplugged; and dramatic temperature changes have been reported throughout the Artist House.

In some of the more exciting encounters visitors see the image of a woman in a wedding dress on the staircase, or awake to an apparition hovering over their bed in the middle of the night. Some have even reported conversations with the ghost of a lady who, though happy with the way her house has been taken care of, would like to see a particular set of drapes changed.

More than a few people have had shivers travel up their spine as they observe the house from outside and a shade mysteriously lifts to reveal the ghostly image of a woman.

Though some believe Robert's spirit has returned to (or possibly never left) the Artist House, they all seem to agree that his energies are confined to the attic room. It is said that when Anne Otto died her spirit returned to protect the house and all guests from any harm. It is her ghost that watches from the window of the turret to see who is arriving, just as she did in her mortal life.

Many theories exist as to why Robert behaves the way he does. Some call it voodoo, others attribute it to an ancient curse, and some believe Gene's ghost has returned to the doll he so loved. Robert is not the first case of an inanimate object taking on a personality, and he is probably not the last. Though we may never know all of the answers surrounding these bizarre circumstances, Robert will always serve as a reminder: Beware of the objects you possess, or one day they may end up possessing you!

The Artist House.

Photo: Rob O'Neal

Geiger's Ghost

Standing on the steps a mere four feet in front of him was the apparition of a woman. She appeared to be in her fifties and was wearing a light blue dress with a full length apron, complimented by frills and a matching white cap. Pete continued to stare in disbelief as she moved back and forth on the step before disappearing completely. "Lucretia?"

Captain John Hurling Geiger.

Photo: Rob O'Neal

"This is the ghost of Captain Geiger," the rugged voice boomed. "Welcome to my house." Gina pushed the stop button on her tape recorder and pulled one side of the headphone set off her ear. She looked at Mandy and watched for her smile. "I guess what they said about the house is true," she laughed. That was Gina's cue to start the tape back up. They had read about the house in *The National Directory of Haunted Places* and wanted to make sure their tapes were synchronized just in case anything strange happened.

The two strolled slowly along the pathways of aged brick which wandered about the bamboo palms and orange jasmine. A variety of wild orchids danced from the fruit trees which towered above the three story conch house. "What a breathtaking place," Gina thought to herself. As she discovered the history which surrounded her it only added to the sense of romance and adventure. Little did she know that the very bricks she was walking on served as grave markers for at least seven people who were buried on the property.

The Audubon house was built by Captain John Hurling Geiger in the 1840's. Both a harbor pilot and master wrecker, Geiger made his fortune in the wrecking industry salvaging goods from the many ships that crashed into the treacherous reef off the Florida Keys. Desiring the finest house on the island, Geiger wasted no time in contracting ship's carpenters to begin construction and soon had a fine family home with spacious, open air verandas providing an ideal place to relax while keeping an eye on the not too distant waters. It was a prime location for a wrecker to call home, and upon completion the house was luxuriously furnished with treasures from the very ships that Geiger had salvaged on the reef.

The narrated history continued, and soon led Gina and Mandy through to the entrance of the house where they met Pete.

"Is this place really haunted?" Mandy asked the gentleman who had issued them their tape players and headphones. His eyebrows raised and a smile came across his face.

"That, ladies, is something you will have to decide for yourselves." As they headed upstairs to the second floor Pete remembered the first ghost he had encountered in the house.

It had been nearly three years since Pete first came to the Audubon House. Some of the other employees had talked about the strange happenings, but it always seemed a joke. The occasional light would flicker or a strange noise would come from an empty room, but nothing ever happened that was so strange it could not be explained by the settling of the house or faulty wiring–at least not until that one morning.

It was about 8:00 a.m. when Pete arrived to prepare the Audubon House for the day's tours. He went about his tasks as usual; turning off the external alarms, inspecting the rooms and opening the porches. As a final task he opened the front door and moved the two antique rockers onto the porch. Pete could not believe his eyes.

Standing on the steps a mere four feet in front of him was the apparition of a woman. She appeared to be in her fifties and was wearing a light blue dress with a full length apron, complimented by frills and a matching white cap. Pete continued to stare in disbelief as she moved back and forth on the step before disappearing completely.

"Lucretia!" Pete said out loud, speaking to no one in particular. He was referring to Mrs. John Geiger, mother of twelve and the lady who had spent most of her life in the Audubon Home. It seemed obvious to him that she had returned to the place she loved most. Though she had disappeared, Pete continued staring where she had been, trying to take in everything he had just seen.

"Which of the plants is the Geiger tree?" the voice asked. Pete snapped back from his memories of the ghostly encounter and motioned to the tree with the orange blooms named by Audubon in honor of Captain Geiger. Gina and Mandy continued touring the house, their hopes of encountering a ghost growing weaker and weaker as they climbed the stairs to the third floor.

"What a creepy looking picture." Gina said, referring to the oil painting of a young boy hanging in the hallway. Tom Henrie, one of the house's managers, was passing by and overheard the conversation.

"That is what's known as an oil-o-gram," Tom volunteered. "Before photographs were readily available, oil paintings were one of the more common ways to preserve a person's image and this applied to both the living and the dead. You see, when someone died, other family members would want to remember them just as they were at that point in time. An artist would be brought in to paint a family portrait and the deceased would be propped up with the rest of the group. Though this helped the artist to capture the group dynamic, making the eyes look life-like proved to be a bit more difficult. Look closely at the eyes of this one and you can tell it is a deceased child."

Mandy squinted her eyes slightly and moved closer to the painting as Gina turned her head away. "How morbid," Gina responded, crinkling her face. "Is it the kid in the picture that supposedly haunts the house?"

"It's a possibility," Tom replied, "but most of the hauntings seem to take place in *this* room." He motioned to the doorway on the left and the three went in.

The room was strange, that was for sure. Antique toys lay spread across the floor as if someone had just finished playing with them and period clothing hung from the hooks as if waiting to be worn that evening. In one corner of the room a baby carriage sat empty, and a large mirror seemed to rock back and forth on the far wall. Mandy looked for a vent that might be causing the draft but saw nothing. The mirror continued to sway.

"You can probably tell by the toys that this was the children's room," Tom continued. "During the days of yellow fever it was used as a quarantine room and was a place that saw a lot of death. In addition to the kids that the Geigers lost to yellow fever, we know that another son died in this room after falling from the almond tree outside.

"People have always reported weird things happening up here. Some employees talk about mysterious foot steps and cold chills, and a few have claimed to see apparitions, but it's the visitors that always comment on how strange the room is. We were getting so many remarks that we decided to paint the room a brighter color. We thought that might take away some of the gloom, but the comments still keep coming."

The girls thanked Tom for his time and continued their tour without incident. As they turned in their cassette players and headphones, Pete inquired about their luck with the ghosts.

"If this place is haunted, the ghosts must be on vacation today," Mandy chimed.

"I'm beginning to think there's no such thing," Gina added.

No sooner had they said this than the empty rocker on the porch began moving to and fro at a steady pace. All heads turned towards the rocker, and then back at each other as if looking for reassurance of what was really happening. "Must be the wind," Pete assured with the same smile and raise of the eye brows he had given before. "Must be the wind." Gina and Mandy managed to produce a nervous smile before turning to leave.

The girls headed back out along the aged brick path, neither one saying a word until they left the gift shop. "Do you think that was really the wind?" Gina asked Mandy. There was a long pause as Mandy tried to make sense of what they had just seen in her own head. "I don't know," she replied. "I just don't know."

Before photographs were readily available, oil-o-grams were used to remember the deceased.

Photo: Rob O'Neal

Beyond the Grave

.

The man stared at them blankly as though he never heard a word they said, but as Brian approached, he turned opaque, then transparent, then disappeared completely right before the couple's eyes. Both stood speechless for a moment and stared ahead as if questioning their own sanity. Maria broke the silence.
"We've got to find Jim!"

The Red Rooster Inn.

Photo: Gregory Hummel

Brian and Maria Delgado could barely contain their excitement as they sped past mile marker four on their way to the southernmost city in the continental United States. It would be the first visit for both of them, but Maria kept feeling as if she had been to Key West before. It was not deja vu, but more of a familiarity; a feeling that she belonged here. The buildings, the water, everything she encountered was what she had envisioned. She even directed Brian to their guest house without using the map they had picked up at the visitor's center.

Her familiarity increased with each passing mile marker, and as they pulled into the drive of the Red Rooster Hotel, it was as if she was back at home in Minnesota. Little did she know how close to home she was.

"You've been listening to too many of your grandmother's stories," Brian laughed as he began to unload their luggage.

Perhaps he was right. Key West was one of her grandmother's favorite topics, but rightfully so. "Nana," as she called her, had grown up in Key West and was descended from some of the island's earliest settlers.

Maria recalled her childhood gathered with her cousins on Nana's front porch listening for hours to her tales of the tough but happy days growing up in the Keys. From ship wrecks to Presidential visits, Nana knew them all; some stories from first hand experience, others she had been told as a child. Maria had always relished the stories, often picturing herself as the main character, but never did she imaginethat the stories would come to life on this vacation.

After check-in, the couple wasted no time jumping into their swim suits and heading towards the pool for a couple of tropical drinks. It was here that they met Jim and Gary, owners of the Red Rooster, and had a brief conversation.

The standard questions were asked. "Is everything O.K. with your room?...First time in the Keys?...etc. Then Maria mentioned the familiar feelings she kept getting.

"It probably has something to do with your name," Jim joked. "This was originally the Delgado family mansion."

Jim began to tell the story of the house. Before becoming the Red Rooster it had served as everything from a flop house and a brothel to affordable apartments for Coast Guard personnel. He went on to explain the Queen Anne style of architecture, but was cut short by a phone call just as he was about to explain the uniqueness of the concrete front porch and the secret of the house that it held.

As the day came to a close Maria and Brian returned to their room to prepare for the sunset celebration. Maria was first in the shower, so Brian kicked back on the bed and thumbed through the tourist guide to see what the town had to offer. The sound of the water turning off signaled Brian that it was his turn, so he tossed the tourist guide to the side and went to his suitcase to get his shower bag.

As Maria came out of the bathroom she was overwhelmed by the rich scent of cigar smoke. Normally the smell would have bothered her, but this seemed different from the cigars Brian and his friends had smoked in the past on poker night. The smell was sweet and smooth instead of overwhelming and rotten. None the less, she did not want him smoking in their room and she made her feelings known.

"Brian, you could at least wait until we get outside to smoke those things. You know how I feel about them!"

"It's not me," Brian insisted, holding his hands in the air to show that they were empty.

"Maybe it's someone outside?"

Brian opened the door, but the hallway was empty. The smell vanished just as suddenly as it had appeared. "Strange," he thought.

The scent reminded Maria of Nana's stories about their ancestors who worked the cigar trade in Key West long before the current wave of popularity arose. "Perhaps it was one of them coming to check up on me," Maria thought to herself, half joking, but half serious. As they headed out for the evening she asked one of the staff at the front desk if he had noticed anyone with a cigar in the area, but

26

he had seen nothing. Again Maria put her thoughts to the side.

After sunset it was straight to Sloppy Joe's for drinks and dancing. After a couple of hours both were getting tired so they decided to call it a night and hopped a jitney back to the Red Rooster. As they entered their room the scent of cigar smoke was present again, but just as before it disappeared quite suddenly. Maria was too tired to worry about it and climbed right into bed, but the sweet smell was too alluring for Brian, so he headed out to the pool for a stogie of his own. It was shortly after he left that Maria awoke.

It was not the sound of the door opening that awakened Maria, but the cigar smell which she was becoming all too familiar with. This time she was sure it was Brian, but rather than get frightened by his childish prank, she decided to ignore him and pretend to sleep. After a few minutes of silence and cigar smoke, Maria felt Brian's weight as he sat down on the bed beside her, and still feigning sleep she rolled over a bit to flop her arm onto his leg. Brian was not there. She opened her eyes and stared in disbelief at the impression on the mattress. Someone or something was sitting there, but it was definitely not her husband.

Maria started to scream and the door swung open. It was Brian "What's wrong honey?" he asked.

"Something was sitting on the bed and the cigar smell was back and he was right here and..."

Brian rushed to her side and put a comforting arm around her shoulder. "Don't worry honey, you were just having a bad dream. No one is in the room except me and the cigar smell is probably just coming from the vents."

Maria continued pointing to the mattress where the impression had been, but nothing remained.

"You were just having a bad dream," Brian assured.

Maria calmed down and was eventually able to get back to sleep.

The next morning the couple ran into Jim and Gary at breakfast. Maria started talking about her strange experiences with the cigar smoke, and Brian once again brushed it off as coming through the vents. Upon hearing their story, Jim and Gary gave each other a knowing look and explained that the house was haunted. Brian and Maria were not the first ones to report the sweet scent of cigars.

Jim picked up his story where he had left off the first time and went on to tell about the Delgado family.

"It was during the late 1800's that the cigar business began booming in Key West and the Delgados were one of the largest manufacturers. The Red Rooster was built around 1870 and it served as the Delgado family home for a number of years. It is the ghost of Mr. Delgado that is supposed to be the cause of the hauntings, and the sweet, rich cigar scent is said to have been his favorite brand.

Maria and Brian listened carefully as the story continued. Once again Jim got to the part about the mystery of the porch and the secrets it held when he was called away. Jim promised to finish the story before they headed back to Minnesota.

The subject of ghosts continued to arise for the remainder of the day. Maria was convinced that it was the ghost of Mr. Delgado who had joined her in bed the previous night, but Brian remained skeptical about the whole situation insisting that it was nothing but a dream and there were no such things as ghosts. He laughed even more at the thought that this could be one of Maria's ancestors.

Though there were many Delgados descended from Key West, Maria could not help but think there was some connection. Her mind searched for one of Nana's stories that would make sense of the situation, but the only Delgado of any relation from the cigar industry was her great grandfather's brother, and he had died in Cuba, which ruled out any possibility of haunting a house in Key West. Even if it was not a relative, Maria was anxious to hear the rest of the story and find out the mystery of the front porch. Maria told Brian she wanted to return to the Red Rooster for a nap before dinner, but she was really hoping to find Jim.

Gary's coffee shop in the front of the hotel made the perfect place for the couple to keep watch. Brian sipped on his short espresso and talked about his plans to meet Jimmy Buffett, but Maria heard none of his conversation. She had her head down, staring at the patterns of the concrete porch, looking as if she expected the floor to start talking. After twenty minutes of this they went to their room.

"What are you doing here?" Maria asked the old Cuban gentleman standing at the foot of her bed.

"This is an occupied room, you can't be in here," Brian insisted.

The man stared at them blankly as though he never heard a word they said, but as Brian approached he turned opaque, then transparent, then disappeared completely right before the couple's eyes.

Both stood speechless for a moment and stared ahead as if questioning their own sanity. Maria broke the silence. "We've got to find Jim!"

After a brief search, Jim was located next door in the adjoining gardens of the Chelsea House. The three walked around to the front of the house and sat down for coffee before Jim proceeded with the story.

"I mentioned to you about the Delgado family living here for many years. Well it seems that Mr. Delgado mysteriously disappeared one October, never to be seen again. His wife told neighbors he had gone to Cuba to take care of some business for the cigar company and would be back soon, but the days became months and the months became years and still no sign of Mr. Delgado.

"Many people in town assumed him to be dead, while a few others believed he had run off with a mistress. No one suspected foul play, and all of them felt sorry for Mrs. Delgado. The funny thing was, she never accepted the pity. It would only be found out later why she had avoided the attention.

"As she lay on her death bed, Mrs. Delgado confessed to murdering her husband. She claimed to have buried him under the house, but passed on before the exact location could be discovered.

"A search of the grounds and under the house was conducted, but no body was found. As a last resort the wooden front porch was removed and the area beneath searched. Still no body. Mr. Delgado's remains were never found.

"The original porch was replaced with the current concrete version. It was in the 1950's that the ghost stories started circulating, but for the past ten years the majority of the hauntings seem to take place in October. Some people think it has to do with Halloween, but we are pretty sure that it coincides with Mr. Delgado's disappearance.

"Some people claim he is returning to reveal the true location of his body. Others say that, like many ghosts, he does not know he is dead. Whichever the case, someone's ghost returns each October, and many Conchs in town refer to the concrete porch as the largest grave in Key West."

Maria phoned Nana that evening to share the amazing chain of events that had happened to her. When she got to the part about Mr. Delgado being buried under the house, Nana went silent. After a long pause Maria asked her if she was all right.

"Stranger things have happened in Key West my dear," she replied. "Stranger things have happened."

The Doctor's Inn

"Amy tossed and turned until all she could do was stare at the door, listen to the echo of the steps and watch the shadow that the person was casting as his feet blocked the light of the hallway which was visible under the crack of the threshold. With each round they seemed to pause by her door a little bit longer than the time before."

The Eaton Lodge.

Photo: Rob O'Neal

A loud thud startled Amy from her sleep. She was usually a light sleeper, used to being called at all hours as a paramedic; but tonight she had fallen into an unusually deep sleep from which she had trouble emerging. After looking around for a moment trying to figure out where she was, her senses returned. "Key West. Eaton Lodge. Doctor's office." she said aloud as she groped for her watch on the night stand. "Doctor's office? Where did that come from?" It was then that Amy remembered her dream.

Though it started to fade fast, she recalled the image of the office. The patient was lying on the table with the doctor standing over him. Amy stood beside the doctor looking down at the patient as well, but the situation was bad. Although Amy knew the patient could be treated, the doctor did not seem to understand what was wrong. The more she tried to explain, the less he understood. Eventually he ignored her completely and began walking back and forth. It was when the doctor began pacing that Amy woke up.

A thud echoed in the hallway a second time, then a third. After a brief pause it went back in the other direction. Someone was pacing in the hallway and by the sound of it, they had very big feet. Amy realized now why the doctor had been pacing in her dream, and laughed at the subliminal suggestion. She had now found her watch and by squinting her eyes she could see it was nearly two in the morning.

"Sounds like someone had a good night," she thought, rolling over and closing her eyes to go back to sleep. The footsteps continued for about five more minutes, each time stopping what seemed to be a little bit closer to the front of her door. Amy tossed and turned until all she could do was stare at the door, listen to the echo of the steps and watch the shadow that the person was casting as his feet blocked the light of the hallway which was visible under the crack of the threshold. With each round they seemed to pause by her door a little bit longer than the time before. All types of thoughts started circling Amy's mind before she decided to put a stop to it all.

Enough was enough. Amy quietly stepped out of bed and walked to the doorway. The footsteps were moving away from the door. As her hand gripped the door knob, the foot steps returned in her direction until she was sure they were just inches away. She took a deep breath; and timing the moment perfectly, swung the door open and gave her best "what the heck are you doing stalking around outside my room at two in the morning" look–but it was to no avail. The hallway was empty. No footsteps; no person; no nothing.

Amy shook her head in disbelief. Somebody or something was out there and she was sure of it. After a thorough inspection of the hallway and public areas she went back to her room. She stayed awake for another hour waiting for the noise to return, but eventually drifted off to sleep. The following morning at breakfast she struck up a conversation with the people in the room next door.

"Late night last night?" Amy asked, hoping to discover the source of last night's disturbance.

"No not really," Leslie replied. "We were probably in by midnight."

"Well, did you hear anything strange? Any funny noises?"

"No, we slept like babies all night long."

Amy went on to explain the footsteps and the heavy pacing. Leslie's eyes widened.

"That's what Jack and Jana heard, only they said it was coming from the room above them!" she exclaimed. Amy breathed a sigh of relief.

"At least I'm not the only one who heard them last night then…I was beginning to think I was going crazy."

"This wasn't last night," Leslie clarified. "Jana and Jack are friends who came down with us last year. They were staying in the same room you're in. Jana said she couldn't sleep because of all the noise in the room above, but when Jack went and asked them to quiet down, he found the room was empty. We didn't think anything of it– at least not until now."

Amy tried not to think anything of it either. She went out for an afternoon of snorkeling and then took in a show at the Red Barn Theater. After the show she returned to the Eaton Lodge and went to sleep. It was a peaceful night. No footsteps outside the door, no shadows, just a perfect night's sleep.

In the morning when she awoke, Amy was well rested. It was probably the best night's sleep she had experienced in years. The bed was so comfortable that she decided to stay in for another hour, and as her thoughts began to wander the previous night's dreams popped in and out of her head.

"The same Doctor!" she thought to herself. It was the same dream as the night before. This was something she had heard about but never experienced first hand. Her curiosity roused her out of bed and she wondered if the dream was supposed to be telling her something. If it was, she could not figure it out.

After a warm shower and a cup of coffee in the B&B's tropical garden, Amy went out for a day of touring museums. Her first stop was just a couple of blocks away and after exploring the house she started talking with the owner. Somewhere in the conversation she mentioned staying at the Eaton Lodge, and found that he was the former owner. Edward began talking about the beautiful gardens on the property and explained that Genevieve Warren was one of the founding members of the Key West Garden Club. He talked briefly about the architecture and style, commenting that it was a fine home for Gen and the doctor.

"What doctor?" Amy interrupted, thinking back to her dream.

"Dr. Warren," Edward replied. "The Eaton Lodge served as his family home and his doctor's office."

"Which part of the house was his office?"

Edward thought for a minute before his reply. "It would have been in the South East quadrant of the building. If one were facing the house it would be the right half of the building on the lower floors."

Amy let out a nervous laugh. "That's where my room is. I've been having these weird dreams about a doctor."

"Perhaps his ghost has come back to visit you," Edward responded.

"Ghost?" she asked. "Is the place haunted?"

"Some people think so. I believe that Genevieve still has a presence in the house, but different people say different things. Many people report heavy pacing and attribute it to Doctor Warren. They think he is walking back and forth worrying about his patients. Some joke that the spirit is an unfortunate patient, hanging around waiting for a second opinion."

"What does the doctor look like?" Amy asked, thinking she may have discovered the meaning of her dream.

Edward did not know, but referred her to the library. "The photo archive contains pictures of many of the town's prominent citizens. That would be a good place to check."

Amy thanked Edward for his time and headed to the library. Looking through the photo index she saw a long list of Warrens. As she neared the end of the list she prepared herself for disappointment, but then the name stood out. Warren, Dr. William. File # 280, #3259.

She requested the album from the historian. As he emerged from the walk in vault with the open book, Amy nearly fainted. Though the photo only gave a side view, she could tell right away that the man in the picture was the doctor who had appeared in her dreams.

The historian noticed her reaction. "You look like you've seen a ghost."

"I think I have," Amy responded.

Doctor Warren in his pre-haunting days.

Photo: courtesy of Monroe County Public Library

Night Nurse

*...I was startled awake by something icy cold on my forehead.
I opened my eyes to see the image of a large lady standing over my
bed. One hand was stretched across my forehead as if checking for a
fever and the other on my wrist checking for a pulse. I tried to pull
my arm away but was unable to move. Next I tried to scream but
nothing came out...*

The Mercedes Hospital, then...

Photo: Courtesy Monroe County Library

and now.

Photo: Gregory Hummel

Ghosts of Key West

Larry Stanford did not believe in ghosts. It was not that he had anything against the paranormal, but his scientific and mathematical background could not offer any explanations for their existence so he did not believe.

Larry was originally from Connecticut. During college he majored in business finance and played baseball on a scholarship, eventually going pro. When his career was cut short due to a shoulder injury he turned to investment banking, but quickly tired of the corporate world and retired to Key West at the age of twenty-seven. Tending bar would be a good way to pass the time and earn a little bit of money on the side as well.

The Gato House seemed like a good place to live. Though it was not in the heart of old town, it was pretty close, and a bicycle would get him anywhere he needed in no time. The rent was reasonable and the neighborhood seemed quiet. With eleven other units in the building it would provide a good opportunity to meet people, and with tourist season just around the corner apartments were going fast. He signed a lease and moved in the same day. After settling in he called home to brag about the warm weather and how tough it was getting used to living in paradise. His Mom answered the phone.

"Hello?"

"Hey Mom, it's me."

"Larry! How are things in Key West?"

"Not bad. No job yet, but I found an apartment and just got moved in."

"That's great, what's it like?"

"Well it's called the Gato house and it's kind of like a giant house that was turned into apartments. I'm up on the second floor near the back. It's a pretty cool place."

"Gato? That's Spanish for cat. Your not living in a cat house are you?"

Larry laughed. He had never even thought about the translation of the word, though now it made him wonder if the building had ever served such a purpose. He finished his conversation, laughed at the

40

thought again and then headed out for a newspaper.

Scanning the want ads for a bartending job proved fruitless. Moving all day had taken its toll, so Larry kicked back on the couch and closed his eyes. What a great feeling it was not to worry about setting an alarm. When he awoke it was dark out, so rather than going out for a night on the town he decided to spend his first evening alone in his new apartment.

Three sharp raps on the door startled Larry from his thoughts. He opened the door to find a man about the same age holding two bottles of beer in his hand. "Welcome to the neighborhood. I'm Kip from next door." Larry invited Kip in and the two began talking. Larry brought up the name "cat house" and asked if it had any significance to the building, but Kip explained that the name Gato was quite common in Key West and that the building had in fact been a hospital for the poor. In literal translation the place was once called "Casa del Pobre".

"A poor hospital. That should make my mom happy."

"Just make sure you don't tell her that it's haunted," Kip warned.

Larry looked back with a look that said 'you've got to be joking,' but Kip assured him this was no laughing matter.

"It's haunted by a lady named Maria. She used to work in the hospital."

Larry did not believe, but was curious to hear the stories about the place he was to call home for the next year. "Let me start from the beginning," Kip said.

"As I told you, the house was originally known as the Casa del Pobre, or house of the poor. A lady named Maria Valdez de Gutsens served as the administrator of the hospital from 1911 to 1941. Maria was the life blood of the hospital, and many of the people who knew her described her as a saint.

"As for her appearance, most of the people in the building can vouch that she is a short, stocky woman with long white hair that has been pulled back from her face into a large bun."

"You mean she *was* a short stocky woman?" Larry questioned.

"No. I mean *is*. Like I told you, she still haunts the house. But back to the story.

"Maria used to work long hours taking care of the administrative duties in the hospital. As they were often short staffed, Maria would spend her spare time assisting with various nursing duties such as taking temperatures, changing bed sheets, and other simple tasks. When this was finished, instead of taking a break she would stand on the street corners soliciting donations and when payday came for the cigar workers she would often go door to door ensuring that the hospital received the funds it needed to stay in operation.

"Maria worked in the hospital until her death in 1941. The hospital closed down the following year, but even before that there was evidence that her ghost never left the building. The following story has been recounted by various residents of the Gato House for many years.

"A couple of months after the death of Maria de Gutsens, a man was checked into the hospital with severe pneumonia. Convinced of his pending death, but unable to move on his own, he thought of his wife and kids and lamented over the fact that he would die without being able to express his love to them one last time. As he lay suffering in the middle of the night, a nurse appeared at his bedside and asked if she could be of any assistance. He requested her help in penning a letter to his family and she happily obliged. The two stayed together for about an hour; the man lying in bed and dictating the letter, the nurse patiently writing out the words until he was finished. Upon completion she inserted the letter into an envelope, addressed it and placed it on the window sill beside his bed. She then stayed by his side until he fell asleep.

"The following morning the man awoke and his condition had improved significantly. When the nurse conducted her rounds in the morning the gentleman asked if she would summon the night nurse so that he could thank her. 'I was the only one here all night,' she replied, to which the man went on to describe the nurse who had helped him. "She was a short, stocky lady with white hair and a blue-gray dress." The nurse recognized the description. "We used to have a lady here that looked like that, but she has since passed on." The man was insistent that she had been there and pointed to the letter that she had helped him to pen.

"The nurse picked up the letter and stared in disbelief at the envelope. It was Maria's handwriting."

"Great story," Larry said, "but I don't believe in ghosts."

"You will," Kip replied, "you will."

The next morning Larry decided to get an early start. As he was leaving he ran into Adriana in the court yard. She introduced herself as one of the downstairs neighbors and the two had a brief conversation. Larry was about to excuse himself when he decided to ask her about the ghost.

"Did you experience her already?" Adriana asked in disbelief. Larry assured her he had not, but that Kip had been telling him some stories. Adriana offered to share her experience, so Larry joined her at the table to listen.

"I had been living here for about three months and never heard anything about a ghost. For that matter, I never even knew the place was a hospital. I thought it was a cat house like the name said."

Larry laughed and explained his mother thought the same. Adriana continued.

"The flu was going around and I got hit pretty hard by it. I eventually ended up spending two days in bed. I had a temperature of about 102° and managed to sleep O.K. for awhile, but the first night I was startled awake by something icy cold on my forehead. I opened my eyes to see the image of a large lady standing over my bed. One hand was stretched across my forehead as if checking for a fever and the other on my wrist checking my pulse. I tried to pull my arm away but was unable to. Next I tried to scream but nothing came out. I think she sensed I was frightened because she suddenly disappeared."

"That's pretty strange," Larry agreed, "but I don't believe in ghosts."

"There's more," Adriana continued.

"The next night I awoke again to the icy chill on my forehead and Maria standing by my side. I had told Julie next door of the previous night's experience and she told me about her encounters with the ghost and the story of Maria. Knowing the story, I was not as frightened, but it was still quite a shock waking to find this. Again Maria sensed my fear and disappeared, but she returned three times that night. On her third arrival I built up the courage to speak and told Maria I appreciated what she was doing, but that she was frightening me. She took a step back from the bed, gave me an understanding smile and faded away. I have never seen her since."

"Great story," Larry thought to himself, but he attributed the ghostly visions to her fever. "Ghosts don't exist," he told himself again.

The following months brought about many changes. Larry secured a job in one of the many Duval Street clubs, and he was getting to know a lot of people in Key West. Though he continued to hear stories about the ghost of Maria from other tenants in the building, he had pretty much convinced himself that they were all pulling his leg. It was about this time that by some strange coincidence he met Howard.

Howard had been in Key West for nearly twelve years. The bar at which Larry worked was one of his favorite watering holes, so he made sure to introduce himself with the hope of gaining free drinks in the future.

The discussion went as many in the Keys do. How long have you lived here? Where are you from? Do you like the Keys? Somehow the fact that Larry was in the Gato House came up and a bond was formed.

"I used to live there!" Howard exclaimed. "Have you met the ghost?"

Larry explained to Howard that he did not believe and Howard went on to tell his story.

"I lived in the house about three years ago. My room was toward the front overlooking the courtyard. One afternoon, and we're talking broad daylight, the image of a woman appeared in the center of my room. Though I should have been frightened, it wasn't scary at all.

"One of the first things I noticed was that she was not alone. The ghost of a man appeared with her but he stayed near the door. He was dressed like an engineer or a maintenance man, and I got the feeling that the two had some kind of relationship. He acted as though he was fixing the door knob and kept looking over his shoulder as if checking to see that Maria was all right.

"A sad look seemed to come over Maria's face, so I asked her if she was O.K. She nodded her head and said, "Yes. I am fine." I then asked if there was anything I could do for her, but she just shook her head back and forth slowly. 'No, no. No, no.' After that the two of them disappeared. I saw her appear alone once more before I moved out. She was walking down the staircase and gave me a smile as she faded away."

Larry bought Howard a beer and thanked him for his story. He started to wish he would have an encounter so that there would be reason to believe. It seemed like the ghost appeared to everyone in the building except him and he was starting to feel left out.

With October came Fantasy Fest. Larry had heard the comparisons to Mardi Gras, but never expected a small town could put on such a big party. He was even more amazed at the attraction his house had become for the week of Halloween, with the constant flow of traffic outside hoping to get a glimpse of the ghost. As the island became more crowded, so did Larry's apartment. Three of his friends from Connecticut came down to stay, and because of the lack of hotel rooms ended up staying on his floor.

Larry returned home one night to find them all home. "I thought you would all be at the bar by now," Larry said as he headed to the fridge to grab a soda.

"You're not going to believe what happened," his friend Joey replied. "We think we saw a ghost!" Larry laughed and mentioned that everyone thinks the place is haunted. Joey explained what had happened.

"We were sitting around having a couple of beers before we went out when the whole room got kind of cold. Right in the middle of the room there appeared a column of silvery sparkles like the kind you would see on Star Trek when someone's about to get beamed up. It stayed there for about five seconds and then it seemed to snap back into a ball the size of a grapefruit and disappeared completely. I'm not crazy either, we all saw it." The other two nodded their heads in agreement and Larry told them all about Maria.

At the end of the year Larry moved into another apartment closer to town. Though he never saw the ghost of Maria he continued to hear stories from other residents. Most of them told of pulses being taken and temperatures checked. A few reported a sparkling light like his friends had seen. Though Larry does not doubt what the others have seen, he still does not believe in ghosts. Key West is very haunted, Larry. One day you will...

Maria De Gutsens.

Photo: courtesy Monroe County Library & Rob O''Neal

The Oldest Ghost

"The noise started off right at the top of the stairs and made a spinning sound like glass marbles do on a wooden floor. I was a little bit frightened but decided to go take a look. As I rounded the corner to the staircase, I expected to see the floor covered with marbles, but it was bare. It was then that I looked upstairs, and there she was; a little girl surrounded in a white glow playing marbles on the floor of the hallway."

The oldest house in Key West.

Photo: Gregory Humme

Creeeak, thunk! Creeeak, thunk! Creeeak, thunk! Charles was all too familiar with the sounds of the antique rocking chair coming from the room above. The weight of someone sitting in the rocker caused the floorboards to creak each time the chair went back and the thunk was the result of a slightly uneven rail. None the less, Charles felt obliged to get out of bed and make sure things were in order. It was part of his job after all.

He switched on the bedside lamp and looked at the old grandfather clock–two in the morning, same as the nights before. Charles sat up in bed and stretched a bit before climbing out from under the covers.

Most people would have been a bit reluctant to walk around the darkness of such a strange place in the middle of the night, but Charles wasn't bothered. It was probably his experiences in the war that made it so easy; but then again, he was not a superstitious man so ghosts were nothing to be afraid of.

As he slipped on his sandals and grabbed a flashlight from beside the bed, Charles noticed the sound was getting louder. Creeeak, thunk! Creeeak, thunk! He rounded the corner and began to ascend the staircase with a slow, steady pace, paying no mind to the old oil portraits lining the wall that watched his every move. The rocking chair continued. Creak, thunk! Creak, thunk! As he entered the master bedroom and aimed the light at the chair, everything came to a stop. No one was in the rocking chair. No one was in the room. No one was in the house. Charles was alone.

These seemingly strange events came as no surprise to Charles. He had gone through the same thing dozens of times and always found the same results. The windows were sealed up tightly, eliminating the possibility of a draft. But even if they had been open, the chair was so heavy it would have taken a pretty strong gust to get any movement. Besides that, it would take a very unique wind gust to rock the chair in both directions.

Charles had only told one person about the strange occurrence. It was his cousin Joe, but Joe just laughed and told him rats were to blame. Charles knew better. As he turned to go downstairs and get back to sleep he looked at the portrait of Francis Watlington. "Don't you worry Captain, I'm just looking after your place," he said aloud. "No need for you to be up worrying about things." Charles laughed at himself as he said this. "Talking to ghosts?" he thought. "Old man, you're going crazy." He returned to his room and went back to sleep. The house remained quiet until morning when the alarm clock rang.

It was the start of another day at the Oldest House in South Florida. After taking a quick shower and slipping into his uniform, Charles began to walk from room to room making sure everything was in order. He checked the garden for fallen palm fronds, hung the flags out front and then opened the doors to the public.

A lone man in his sixties was the first to come in. As it turned out he was not there for a tour, but rather to see the place he had called home for so many years. He introduced himself to Charles. "My name is Tod, I used to be the caretaker here."

Charles shook his hand heartily and they exchanged small talk. Charles offered to show him around the place, but Tod politely declined in favor of a self-guided tour. Not much had changed in the eight years since he had left. After fifteen minutes of exploring his old residence, Tod returned to the main entrance and thanked Charles. As he started walking away he paused and turned, but then shook his head and continued. He turned a second time, walked back and looked at Charles. "This is going to sound a little weird, but has anything strange happened to you here?"

Charles looked back at him and thought about the previous night's experience. "That depends on what you mean by strange."

"Well I know your room is just below the main bedroom and I just thought you might have heard something."

"Like the rocking chair?" Charles asked raising an eyebrow.

Tod's eyes opened wide. "You have heard them!"

A common bond was formed and the conversation started to flow. Tod was convinced ghosts were responsible, and even claimed to know who they were. Charles questioned if it could really be spirits from the past. "But if it were I'd have to say it's Captain Watlington." That wa when Tod mentioned the kids.

"One night I was awakened by a very different noise. I had become familiar with the rocking chair sound, but this wasn't even close. I lay in bed for a few minutes trying to figure out what it was, when it dawned on me that someone was playing with marbles.

"The noise started off at the top of the stairs and made a spinning sound like glass marbles do on a wooden floor. Next they started rolling down the staircase one step at a time. Just when one marble stopped, another one would start across the floor and then down the steps. I was a little bit frightened, but decided to go take a look. As I rounded the corner to the staircase I expected to see the floor covered with marbles, but it was bare. It was then that I looked upstairs and there she was; a little girl surrounded in a white glow playing marbles on the floor of the hallway.

"As soon as she saw me she ran into the bedroom. I climbed the stairs to see if she was real, but could find no one. As I left the bedroom, the rocking chair let out that familiar sound. Creeeak, thud! Creeeak, thud! I decided to leave them alone and went back to my room for the night."

Charles had never heard the marbles. A slight chill swept through him at the thought. A few more people came into the museum, so Tod said goodbye and Charles thanked him for the stories. A young lady asked some questions about the house and Charles gave her the full history.

"The Watlington family resided here for a majority of the time," he explained. "Captain Francis Watlington arrived in Key West in 1828 and found employment as both a harbor and coastal pilot, as well as a wrecker. Though his career included such titles as Customs Inspector, Captain of the Sand Key Lightship, Captain of the government schooner *Activa*, member of the Florida House of Representatives, and 'Lieutenant of War' under Key West hero and Secretary of the Navy for the Confederacy, Stephen Mallory–today Watlington is better known for this house, which he lived in since 1834."

"The house was built in 1829, just eight years after the treaty with

Spain which ceded East Florida and the Keys to the United States for unpaid debts. Since then it has seen and survived pirates, wars, hurricanes and fires. The house is most commonly described as a 'New England Bahama House' and it is believed to be the oldest house on the island."

"Tell me more about the Watlingtons," the young lady asked.

"Well, the Captain lived here with his wife Emeline. They had nine daughters but two died at a young age. The remaining seven can be seen in the picture on the wall there. The Captain's family was from St. Croix, but he was born in New York City around 1804. He first learned about shipping in the New York Harbor, which led to his career in Key West."

The day continued much the same. Charles loved answering questions about the house, and when the people had a sincere interest it made him feel even better. It was a busy day, and before he knew it closing time had arrived. As he took down the flags and closed up the doors of the house, his conversation with Tod kept going through his mind. Charles was now beginning to believe he was not alone in the house.

As dusk fell over the island, he prepared for bed wondering what the night would bring. The house was quiet, almost too quiet, and not a sound was heard from the spirits for nearly a month. No rocking chair creaking, no marbles dancing across the floor and down the stairs. Charles actually started to miss the nightly visits, but he kept this to himself in order to avoid the looks. Tod had been the only one so far who did not look at him strangely when he brought up ghostly possibilities, so he avoided the topic all together. Besides, the house had so many fascinating things to discuss that ghosts were the last thing that should come to mind anyway.

Two months had gone by since the last rocking chair incident on the day that Tracy came to the house. She would have passed right by, but her daughter Elizabeth begged her to go in and see the wreckers' display. Tracy obliged, but immediately upon entering was overcome by a strange feeling. She began to walk around the house in a slow, but concentrated manner. As she went from room to room it was as if she was being led rather than directing herself. Tracy's motions continued as she went up the stairs, but when she came back down she was a different person.

"Did you know there is a presence in the house?" she asked Charles.

Taken slightly aback, he laughed and told her there were rumors of ghosts. Tracy began to walk around the room again and came to a stop in front of a large oil painting hanging on the parlor wall. "This is her," she said staring intensely at the portrait. "She likes to stay in the bedroom upstairs where her girls are."

"That's Emeline Watlington," Charles added. "She had nine daughters that lived here with her."

"This one is just a little girl," Tracy continued. "She became quite ill and there was nothing that could be done. Her mother rocked her back and forth for hours until she eventually passed on. Both spirits remain here today."

Charles' voice softened. "Emeline lost two daughters at a very early age."

Tracy walked away from the picture and headed to the door with her daughter. "You are very lucky to have such a caring spirit around you," she said to Charles. "Don't worry about what the others are saying, you know in your heart what is true."

Charles did not quite understand what she was saying, but thinking about it again as he lay in bed that night, he realized what Tracy said was true. "Good night Emeline," he shouted to the room up above. After a few moments of silence her response came back. Creeeak, Thunk! Creeeak, Thunk!

Hard Rock Hauntings

The Curry fortune continued to dwindle, and in an effort to maintain what was left they departed from Key West, selling Robert's home to the Key West Order of Elks. The year was 1920 and though the Elks were pleased to acquire such a fine building, they were soon to find out that the original owner had never left.

When it comes to ghosts lurking about the Hard Rock Cafe most people expect to hear the tender ballads of Elvis Presley or the colorful poetry of Jim Morrison. But anyone who reads the weekly tabloids knows that they are both still alive and kicking. To discover the real spirit of the Southernmost monument to Rock & Roll we have to take a step back in time to the early days of settlement in Key West. Back to the days of William Curry.

William Curry was Florida's first millionaire. Best known for his Victorian mansion that towers over Caroline Street (and rumored to house a few ghosts of its own) William was responsible for many of the town's early structures, as well as the one now occupied by the Hard Rock Cafe.

It was built as a wedding gift for his son Robert and his bride, and the unique architecture is testament to the fact that no expense was spared in construction.

Robert's story is a sad one. Most accounts describe him as a sickly man stricken by asthma, and in addition to his deteriorating health he was the victim of declining fortune. Combined with the pressures of life, all of this was enough to make him despondent and in the summer of 1917 Robert Curry committed suicide. He was found hung to death in the second floor bathroom.

The Curry fortune continued to dwindle, and in an effort to maintain what was left they departed from Key West, selling Robert's home to the Key West Order of Elks. The year was 1920, and though the Elks were pleased to acquire such a fine building, they were soon to find out that the original owner had never left. The first encounter was recalled by a former custodian.

"I had been working in the house for just a couple of months. It was always a little creepy being there at night, but that's to be expected in a place so large when you're all by yourself.

"So I was down on the first floor polishing the handles on the slot machines when I heard a horrible clatter coming from the second floor. Well at first I thought something might have fallen over, but as I got upstairs and saw the overturned table I began to get a little nervous.

This was a pretty big table and no gust of wind was gonna' turn it over like that. I started to get a little frightened thinking someone had broken in, so I turned on all the lights; but looking around I discovered the place was empty.

"That was enough for me. I started cleaning up real quick so that I could get out of there and that's when the footsteps started. They were coming from the storage area on the third floor and they paced back and forth from one side to the other in a slow, steady manner. Not like someone who's expecting a baby, but more depressed like. The door leading up there was still locked, so I knew that this was no burglar. I got out of there as quick as I could and let Mr. Curry have the house to himself for the night.

"The footsteps started happening regularly, so one night I just shouted up to Mr. Curry that I wasn't here to do him any harm. If he left me alone, I'd leave him alone. The footsteps pretty much stopped after that for me, but some of the others here still kept hearing him. That's just Mr. Curry I'd tell them. He won't give you any problems."

The Elks eventually left the building and it took on the names of various businesses including The Shell Man and Mario City, Italian restaurant. Though different people came and went, one chose to stay: Robert Curry. Barry Thompson rented a room on the third floor and had a unique experience of his own.

"I moved to Key West when I was thirteen and attended both Junior High and High School here. During the summer months there was not a lot to do, so when the opportunity to see a ghost came about we all jumped at the chance. One of the older kids explained to us about a guy who had killed himself in the old Elks club that now sat vacant and he insisted that some nights you could see the ghost appear in the windows on the third floor.

"Duval Street was not quite as busy in those days, and the booths and vendors at the Porter Mansion were still a few years away, so we used to lie on the grass across from the haunted house and watch for hours, waiting for the ghost to appear.

"We didn't have much luck at first, but there was still a certain excitement to ghost watching. It was certainly better than sitting around home with our parents or riding our bikes around the pier. It never failed that someone would claim to have seen something, but nothing was ever certain until one night in July.

"It was just me, Phil, and Dave that night and the moon was about half full. We had been there for about an hour and were getting ready to go home when we saw something moving in the window at the top and to the left. Phil was in the middle and he nudged me and Dave without taking his eyes away from the figure. What appeared next I can only describe as yellow glowing eyes. I know it sounds silly, but there was a man with both hands on the window sill as if to support his weight and he stared out the window with a yellow iridescent glow in his eyes. He stayed in the window for what seemed like minutes, but in reality was probably only twenty seconds. He didn't seem to walk away, but kind of vanished.

"The three of us compared notes and we had all seen the same thing. Was it a ghost? I don't know. Was it a human? Not like any I've ever seen. All I can tell you is that something strange was up there."

Randy Mathis tells another story of a ghostly encounter in the building. His story takes place just before Mario City took up residence in the house.

"I had just moved to Key West and considered myself very fortunate to have found an apartment on Duval Street in the heart of all the action. I normally would have complained about lugging all of my furniture up three flights of stairs, but this place was too nice to complain.

"When I signed my lease they didn't tell me that someone was living in the house, but I soon found out. After arranging all of my furniture, I began to hang my paintings and posters on the wall. That's when the trouble started.

"The trouble revolved around one picture in particular. It was a print of the Nina, the Pinta, and the Santa Maria going over a waterfall which was meant to be the edge of the world. In a lifeboat trying frantically to get away from the fall were Columbus and another man and the caption at the bottom read 'I told you so!' ".

Robert Curry, not Elvis, is said to haunt the Hard Rock Cafe.
Photo: Rob O'Neal

"I first hung the picture on the wall facing Duval Street. No sooner had I turned around to grab the next painting when I turned around to see the boat painting on the floor. The nail was still in the wall, the glass was not broken, and I had not heard a noise. Though I was sure I had just hung the painting moments ago, I picked it up and placed it on the wall once more. Who knows, maybe I was getting forgetful. The next time I turned around it was on the floor, resting against the wall again. This was getting weird.

"For the third time I placed the painting on the wall and then sat on the couch and watched it. The painting immediately fell to the floor with a loud thud, shattering the glass and cracking the frame. The force with which it fell made it look as if it were pushed.

"All of the other paintings went up fine. I took the boat picture in to get fixed, and about a month later I received a call saying it was ready. When I returned home I hung it on a different wall, just to play it safe, and then went back downstairs to move my car. When I returned the painting was destroyed. Glass broken, frame cracked, poster torn. If it wasn't a ghost that did that, you tell me what."

Hauntings continue to this day. In the Hard Rock Cafe, a flip of the coin often times determines who has to retrieve the kegs from the beer cellar where there is a constant feeling of being watched. In the administrative offices on the third floor, filing cabinet drawers have been known to open and close on their own, and there are the many reports of cold chills in the restrooms on the second floor. This is the very area where Robert Curry killed himself.

Does the ghost scare people away from the Hard Rock? Not at all. Business is booming and the Hard Rock offers the perfect opportunity to get out of the hot Key West sun and take in a little chill…compliments of Mr. Curry.

Dead Men Tell No Tales

"Jimmy knew he must work quickly with nightfall less than an hour away; so throwing caution to the wind, he picked up a portion of the leg bone and tossed it out of the hole. The bone made a soft thud as it hit the ground and was followed by a loud voice. "Stupid boy! You have no idea what you are dealing with!"

*The Pirates' Well at The Heritage House was once frequented by both
pirates and indians. Rumors of buried treasure persist.*

Photo: Rob O'Neal

Piracy has existed since the advent of travel and trade. From the time the first ships started sailing the seven seas, pirates were on hand to pillage them. Captain Henry Keppel wrote, "As surely as spiders abound where there are nooks and crannies, so have pirates sprung up wherever there is a nest of islands offering creeks and shallows, head-lands, rocks and reefs– facilities in short for lurking, for surprise, for attack, for escape."

Such islands were the Florida Keys, and the traffic of the Spanish galleons in the adjacent sea lanes made the tropical location even more lucrative. Loaded with gold, silver, and precious gem stones, the weighted galleons moved slowly along the cost as the rugged pirates hid in their small, quick sailing brigs camouflaged by mangroves. When the right moment arrived to catch the Spaniards by surprise, the pirates would rapidly approach the galleon, hi-jacking the precious cargo and taking prisoners or massacring the crew, depending on their resistance.

Pirates were a fearless group of people. Driven by greed and lack-ing in trust, a pirate would not think twice about slitting a man's throat for a piece of gold or hauling a thief's body over the barnacle encrust-ed keel of his ship. Unspeakable tortures were utilized, though many remain unknown due to the lack of survivors to speak of the bloody tales.

One of the Keys' most notorious pirates was the infamous Black Caesar. Born a Haitian slave, Henri Caesar obtained his freedom by joining a band of pirates who landed to replenish supplies and water. In no time Black Caesar rose to the command of his own band of pirates, with those who knew him saying his deeds and his soul were as dark as his skin. One of Black Caesar's favorite forms of torture involved chaining a man to a large rock during low tide. After hours in the scorching sun, the tides began to change, cooling the victim's blistered skin and providing temporary relief. As the tides continued to rise, the danger turned to drowning as the prisoner was left to a slow death with great struggle. After giving in to the tides, the body was usually devoured by various sea creatures.

Though torture and looting were a big part of the pirate life, another important aspect involved protecting their treasures from the governments, rival pirates and hundreds of others anxious for an early retirement. The best way of doing this was to bury the treasure in a secluded location, and many pirates went to great lengths to ensure the safety of their riches by devising elaborate maps, booby traps, and other diversions. Legend says a common pirate practice was to enlist the help of only one individual when hiding the treasure. Pirates were a lazy bunch when it came to things other than looting and pillaging, so an assistant to help carry the riches and assist in digging a deep hole came in quite handy. Normally promised a percentage of the treasure in exchange for his help, an eager assistant was easily found, never knowing that his greed would ultimately lead to his demise. Some of the young pirates even plotted to return on their own and claim the entire bounty as theirs, but this was rarely the outcome.

After digging a deep hole and lowering in the treasure, the senior pirate would take out his dagger and stab his unsuspecting helper to death; then throw his lifeless body on top of the treasure and often place the traditional gold coins over his eyes. After filling in the hole and concealing the signs of digging, the pirate would begin his solo trip back to the boat.

Why such a ruthless murder? Pirates were not a trusting group of people, and with good reason. The fewer the people who knew the treasure's location, the better. And what better way to ensure silence than with murder? This pirate practice became so wide-spread that it gave birth to the saying "dead men tell no tales."

Another reason for the murders involved superstition. Pirates were firm believers in ghosts, even to the point of enlisting their help in the area of treasure protection. It was widely believed that the dead pirate's spirit would protect the treasure from anyone trying to gain access; first warning them, then actually dragging the treasure deeper into the ground, exhausting the treasure hunters and forcing them to give up. Stories prevail in coastal towns across the country about pirates' treasures and the ghosts who protect them. Two such stories take place in Key West.

Key West was a unique place in the early 1900's. The wrecking industry had come to an end, tin roofs were replacing the old wooden ones and a railroad had just connected Key West to the rest of the United States. Tourism was a new industry, and everything East of White Street in the area now known as new town was undeveloped. With the exception of the railroad tracks, the new town area was ruled by mangroves, tropical palms, cactus, and wild aloe. It made the perfect playground for a twelve year old boy, and the perfect place for a pirate to hide his treasure.

Jimmy Hernandez was a huge fan of pirates. He used to sit on the front porch for hours, mesmerized as his grandfather told tales of Black Caesar, Jean Baptiste Tavernier, Cap'n Lud and other pirates who frequented the Keys. Jimmy especially loved the stories about buried treasure and spent most of his free time daydreaming about the pirate life and discovering treasure of his own.

Like most twelve year olds, Jimmy had friends. Dino Alverez and George Mason were his closest pals, but every one called George "Spiney" Mason because of his pronounced back bone. The boys spent most of their days exploring the mangroves. It was the perfect place to spend the day building forts, throwing stones, and playing "pirate" as they called their version of hide and seek.

On rainy days the boys were forced to stay inside, playing at either Jimmy's or Spiney's house. One day while rummaging around Jimmy's attic, the boys came across a map. "Could it be a pirate's map?" Jimmy wondered. He raced down from the attic to show Grandpa Hernandez what he had found, the other boys following close behind almost unable to contain their excitement. Grandpa glanced at the map and immediately recognized it as a novelty given to the participants at the Pirate's Ball many years before. As he started to break the news to the boys he paused and figured little harm could be caused by the map, and it might provide a nice adventure for the boys. "It just might be an old pirate's map. Looks awful similar to the way Black Caesar used to draw his."

The boys were off. In no time they had grabbed shovels from their parents' houses and met at their regular entrance to the mangroves. After a few minutes of examining the map, Dino said he recognized one of the landmarks and the boys set off with Dino in the lead.

When they finally arrived at the location, Jimmy and Spiney were a bit skeptical, but Dino assured them they were in the right place and pointed out the split in the mangroves where Snake Creek once ran. The boys continued deeper into the brush and before long were at the indicated site. The ground was tough, making the digging difficult, and progress was slow. It soon started getting dark and the boys headed home, disappointed that nothing had been found, but determined to return the next day and continue searching.

As the days turned into weeks, the three boys dug more than seven holes, each one turning up nothing but a bunch of dirt. Then one day as the summer was nearing an end they had a change of luck.

"I've hit something!" Jimmy bellowed from the hole which was now a good five feet deep. The other boys scrambled over to see what it was and the three worked frantically to uncover what turned out to be a wood plank. After enlarging the hole to remove the plank, the boys prepared themselves for the treasures that awaited them below. A few quick tugs and the plank came up. There in the hole was a human skeleton, it's coin covered eyes glaring back at the boys almost as if angered by the human scavengers. Spiney and Dino ran home quicker than a pair of jack rabbits, but Jimmy was determined to reach the treasure. He stayed behind and began the somewhat frightening job of removing the bones.

At first Jimmy tried standing outside the hole and pushing the skeleton away with the shovel. After a number of failed attempts he climbed into the hole hoping to get better leverage. Jimmy knew he must work quickly with nightfall less than an hour away; so throwing caution to the wind, he picked up a portion of the leg bone and tossed it out of the hole. The bone made a soft thud as it hit the ground, and was followed by a loud voice.

"Stupid boy! You have no idea what you are dealing with!"

Jimmy looked around frantically for the source of the voice but no one was around; just Jimmy and the bones. He scurried to climb out of the hole, but continued to lose his footing. It was then that he felt himself being lifted in the air, then thrown nearly six feet and into a nearby cactus. Jimmy got up and ran, never looking behind him. Dino and Spiney laughed at his story, and although his parents questioned how he got stuck with all of those cactus needles, they too refused to believe his pirate tales.

That night Jimmy told the story to Grandpa and the next morning they woke up early and returned to the spot. Grandpa put the leg bone back in the hole, said a quick prayer, and began returning the dirt and rocks to where they had come from. After only a few scoops, Jimmy stopped him and removed the folded, faded map from his pocket. "This belongs to you," Jimmy said, dropping the map into the grave.

The two remained silent as they walked home. Jimmy spent the next two weeks plucking cactus needles from his body, but eventually everything returned to normal. One night, sitting on the porch, Grandpa started telling his pirate tales again. Jimmy quickly changed the subject. He needed no reminding that dead men tell no tales.

The Guardian

Eric's friend Milena was visiting from Miami and the two were watching television when she jumped up screaming. "Oh my God I just saw a foot!"

Eric Koeppen was convinced he was going crazy. He had the normal schoolboy interest in ghosts while growing up, but after hearing so many people doubt his recent experiences he really began to wonder. It all seemed so real.

Eric attended college in Miami and upon graduating moved to Key West to find out where life was taking him. He laughed at the size of his first Key West apartment. The rent was the same as they had paid for an entire house in Miami, but here he was in a fairly small one bedroom cottage paying the price of paradise. What fond memories he had of the house.

Spacious rooms, a swimming pool, central air conditioning and a forty-two foot dock overlooking the canal. It was everything a senior in college could ask for...and more. Splitting the rent with four of his best friends only enhanced the situation. And then there was the ghost.

It all started one night when Eric was watching television with his girlfriend.

"Did you feel that?" Jody asked out of the blue.

"Feel what?" Eric asked.

"The cold chill," she replied as if he should have known the answer.

"You mean the draft?"

"That was no draft!" Jody insisted. "This place is haunted."

Eric sat back and laughed before returning his attention to the television.

"Sure it is, babe. Sure it is."

Eric was doubtful, but in the weeks that followed, he started paying more attention to the temperatures around the house. Though the chills could happen anywhere, it seemed that they were always felt around the television at night. Eric decided to get Dave's opinion.

"Have you noticed any cold chills going around the room?" he asked casually one night during a commercial break from *America's Funniest Home Videos*.

Without missing a beat, Dave replied, "If you want to see cold you ought to try sleeping in my room. Even when it's ninety degrees outside the place is like a refrigerator."

It was true. No matter what the temperature was through the rest of the house, the back bedroom was always at least ten degrees cooler. In addition to that, Ashley, the house cat, refused to go near the back room and even went so far as to marking his territory outside of the bedroom door. Eric started joking with Dave that his room was haunted, but it did not go over well. "With my luck it probably is," he responded. It was clear that Dave was not very fond of ghosts.

Gary was the next one to bring up the possibility of hauntings.

"I think your girlfriend is right about the ghost," he told Eric. Eric turned his head slightly letting Gary know he had his attention. Gary explained.

"Not only is your cat spraying the back hallway all the time, but if you watch him at night sometimes you will see his eyes get really wide as if he is looking at something up in the air. After about ten or fifteen seconds of that he starts to back up like someone is coming at him, and then suddenly he takes off running to the nearest open door trying frantically to get outside. Just yesterday he ran right through the screen door. They say dogs and cats can see these kinds of things and he is definitely seeing something."

What Gary said made sense, and the thought of living in a haunted house didn't sound so bad at first, so they all accepted the possibility and even joked about it from time to time. Burned out light bulbs, doors left unlocked, dirty dishes and more were all blamed on the ghost, but then the apparitions started and things really got weird. J.R told of his encounter one night after dinner.

"I was getting ready for work this morning, and had just come out of the shower. I was heading to my room when I saw a woman walking towards me. I figured she was heading back to Kevin's room, but as she passed by I noticed she was about sixty-five years old. Well, after she passed by, I turned around to see where she was going and as she neared the back bedroom door she completely disappeared. I opened the door to the room to make sure I wasn't going crazy, but she was nowhere to be found."

At this point the discussion turned pretty serious. Everyone started talking about the different encounters and it was decided that the only way to find out for sure was to call the landlady. It was her house and she should know. Eric was nominated to make the call.

"Hello Mrs. Parkinson?"

"Yes."

"This is Eric Koeppen from your house on Oleander."

"Hi Eric, how is everything?"

"Everything is fine, but I was calling because I have a question for you. I don't really know how to ask this, but has anyone ever mentioned that your house might be haunted?"

There was a pause on the line before she responded. "Tell me why you say that, and then I have a story for you."

After hearing Eric explain a few of the things that had given them reason to believe, Mrs. Parkinson arranged to meet with everyone the next day. She arrived just after noon and told them a story that would make them all believers for the rest of their lives.

"My mother died in this house," she started. "Her spirit still remains here." Eric, Dave, J.R., Kevin and Gary all leaned forward in their   chairs listening intently to what she had to say.

"Some people call them ghosts, but I have trouble using that word with my mother. I would have told you about her spirit when you moved in but she had been quiet for a few months beforehand and I thought she may have moved on. You have nothing to be afraid of. My mother was a wonderful woman."

Kay looked up and to the side as if recalling her mother and then turned back to the boys who were anxious to find out more.

"I first realized my mother was still around when her hearing aide started ringing. I had planned on donating it to a charity after her death, so I stuck it in the kitchen drawer until I got around to it. When I heard that high pitched ring coming from the drawer I thought I was going crazy. The hearing aid had no batteries in it, but sure enough, that is where the sound came from. I think it was mom's way of telling me she was still around.

"After that other things started to happen. Mom used to love watching television in the living room at night, so much that it seems she never stopped. On a regular basis after she died I would find the television on in the middle of the night or hear her slippers shuffling across the tile floor to the powder room." Eric made a face at Gary as he recalled the cold chills around the television at night.

"Mom was on everybody's sucker list," she continued. "If people wanted money they sent her something in the mail, and they knew Mom would send a donation. Well one day I went to the mail box and found some mail addressed to her, and upon opening it saw it contained a pen with Mom's name engraved on it. Included was a letter soliciting a donation, and though I kept the pen, the letter and return envelope went right in the trash can. At that moment I heard the most awful shriek coming from Mom's room. I ran back and found the contents of the room scattered everywhere, and seeing this went straight back to the trash can, retrieved the envelope and sent in some money."

The stories continued for about an hour, and when all was said and done the guys felt a little strange knowing that the landlord's mother was haunting their house. Though they all knew it was true, most people who heard the stories listened in disbelief. Eventually everyone stopped talking about the hauntings, and when the lease was up for renewal, each person went their separate ways. It was about this time that Eric moved to Key West and started to experience the other ghost.

The first time Eric saw him he wrote the experience off to an overactive imagination, but the man appeared again and again, sometimes five or six times a day, and never in the same place. He was a tall man, a good six or seven feet, and dressed in a business suit. Though he was always transparent, and mainly seen in Eric's peripheral vision, he moved slowly enough that Eric noticed some other characteristics. The strangest of these was the sandals that he wore on his very large feet.

Convinced that he had lost his mind, Eric told no one of the encounters, and though they continued on a daily basis, he came to accept them as a figment of his imagination. One day that all changed.

Eric's friend Milena was visiting from Miami and the two were watching television when she jumped up screaming. "Oh my God I just saw a foot!"

"What are you talking about?" Eric asked.

"A giant foot just went around the corner into your room."

"What did it look like?"

"It was huge and kind of smoky and I think it was wearing a sandal."

Eric was not imagining things. He told Milena the entire story about the ghost and breathed a big sigh of relief. Things were quiet when Milena returned to Miami, and Eric did not see his ghostly roommate again. Two weeks later he found out why.

"I think he followed me home," the voice on the telephone said.

"Who followed you home?" Eric asked.

"Your ghost. I keep seeing him around my house and in the back seat of my car. It is almost like he's following me around." It was Milena.

Neither one had heard of a ghost moving from place to place, but it was clear that this had happened. Browsing through some new age books at the store, Milena came across an interesting paragraph that spoke of the spirits who appear in suits and move not from place to place, but from person to person. They are the Guardians, it explained, and they go where they are needed most. Perhaps they will one day go with you.

Photo: Gregory Hummel

The Demon Doll

By the end of the day, Bonnie was exhausted and headed back to her hotel for a nap. Though she had looked at hundreds of antiques throughout the house that day, only one came through in her dream. It was the Mrs. Peck doll, and in the dream Bonnie was possessed by the life like child. She and Tom both started to realize there was something strange about this doll.

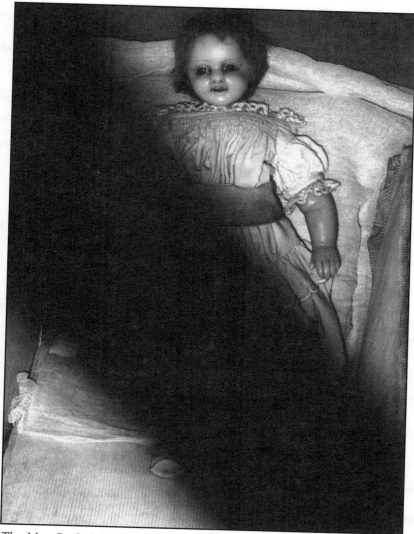

The Mrs. Peck doll did not like being photographed. Many photos turned up thick bars like the one above.

Photo: courtesy of the Audubon House

"We have a possible break-in at the Audubon House," the dispatcher's voice crackled across the police radio. "The manager has been notified and is on the way."

Officer Dixon was the first on the scene. The surrounding gate was still secured, but being only a few feet tall it really didn't provide much security. As backup arrived and went to the rear of the house, Officer Dixon jumped the fence and checked the front door. "Front door is secure," he said into his radio. The officers in back of the house indicated the rear door was locked up tight with no signs of forced entry.

"Must be a false alarm," Officer Dixon thought to himself, stepping back to look for a possible window entrance. It was then that he noticed a small face peering down at him from the window on the third floor. A quick grab for his flashlight proved useless, as no sooner did he make eye contact with the person than they jumped back and disappeared from view. Someone was definitely up there.

"We've got some movement on the third floor," he reported. "Keep a watch on the perimeter and when the manager gets here with the key we'll go check it out." Just then Tom arrived and unlocked the door. Two officers entered the house and proceeded to the third floor, but found no one. They methodically searched the first and second floors as well, but still no burglar. Nothing appeared to be disturbed either, so Tom was brought in to see if he noticed anything missing.

"This is the room where the alarm was triggered," Officer Dixon explained. "It was the heat sensor, so there was definitely someone moving around in here. I saw a face looking down from the window too."

"Is there a chance they could still be in the house?" Tom asked.

"We searched from top to bottom, the place is empty."

"So they got away?"

"I don't see how anybody could...we've had the place surrounded the entire time. Maybe you should have the alarm checked out."

Tom surveyed the children's room, double checking that everything was in place. The Mrs. Peck doll sat in its carriage with an innocent look on her face, but as Tom walked about the room he was sure he saw her eyes following him. "We'll have the alarm company come out tomorrow," he assured Officer Dixon.

The alarm checked out fine, but calls to the police station kept coming in. If it wasn't the silent alarm, it was an eye witness to people moving around; or a concerned neighbor who saw lights going on and off. This continued for months and both Officer Dixon and Tom started growing tired of their 2:00 A.M. meetings. Every time it was the same routine. Motion detected, faces in the window, no one in the house. Though nothing was ever taken, a photo inventory of the house's contents was taken as a precaution. Bonnie Redmond was in charge of the inventory process. Every single item in the house was logged, described and accounted for—well over three hundred items in all, each of which had to be photographed in conjunction with the description. By the end of the day, Bonnie was exhausted and headed back to her hotel for a nap. Though she had looked at hundreds of antiques throughout the house that day, only one came through in her dream. It was the Mrs. Peck doll and in her dream Bonnie was possessed by the lifelike child. She and Tom both started to realize there was something strange about this doll.

Monday morning when the pictures came back from the photo lab, Bonnie began the process of looking through them and cataloging each photo with the necessary information. All of the photos seemed to turn out well, but when she came to the picture of the doll her jaw dropped open. A thick black bar ran from the upper left corner to the lower right. A camera strap seemed like the logical explanation, but the camera she used didn't have one. She went to the room hoping to find something that would have cast the strange image, but it was hopeless. It was as if the doll was saying, "no photos!" A chill ran down Bonnie's spine as she recalled the dream. The Mrs. Peck doll continued to sit in its baby carriage with an innocent look on her face. As Bonnie left the room she could feel its eyes staring at her. She would not be the last.

Visitors began to share their strange experiences with the staff on a regular basis. "Did someone die in the children's room?" some would ask. Others would swear they saw the doll's eyes move. Night time activity reached an all time high, and on many occasions staff would return to the house in the morning to find light bulbs in the house unscrewed from their sockets.

In late 1996 Ernest Watley arrived from England gathering information for a documentary to be aired on the BBC. As he toured the Audubon House he was told about the haunted doll and learned of the troubles people had encountered photographing it.

"Haunted doll?" he laughed. "What a bunch of rubbish." To prove his point Ernest snapped a series of photos. Later that day when Watley left the Audubon house he placed the camera on the passenger seat next to him. As he turned onto US1, the camera casing popped open, causing the film spool to unravel and exposing all of the film. The following day he returned to take more photos but the doll was gone.

In attempts to recover the doll, more information about her came to light. The Mrs. Peck doll stands twenty-two inches in height with a wax head, arms, and legs. Her torso is made of cloth. Dark circles line her eyes and little yellow teeth protrude from her mouth adding to her sickly appearance. She originated in England sometime in the 1850's.

Some stories, though unconfirmed, claim that the maker of the doll searched the whole world over for the perfect model, but by the time the doll was completed the model was deceased. Placing the two next to each other it was impossible to tell which was which according to this story.

Some people believe the doll was possessed by the child. It only seems fitting that the spirit would return to its own likeness. Others claim one of the Geiger children who died of yellow fever in the doll's room may be responsible. All that is certain is that she is gone.

Where did she go? That is unknown. Some people claim she was stolen, others say she left of her own will. The newspapers dubbed her "the demon doll" and say she may still be on the loose.

Since she left the Audubon House, the alarms in her room have stopped going off. Officer Dixon does not come by the house as much, and Tom is sleeping much better at night. The house still has its share of ghosts, but they are better behaved than the Mrs. Peck doll.

A reward still stands for the doll's return. If you have a doll in your house fitting her description, you could be eligible. How can you tell if it is her? Simple. Check for the wax head, arms, and legs, verify a cloth torso, and pay very close attention to her eyes. I think she might be watching you.

His Enemy's Tomb

As the flame illuminated the ground Greg noticed that the marble had suffered years of erosion. Even with the aid of the lighter, the name on the stone was impossible to read. In the middle of the grave was a small section where the marble had caved in, and out of pure, morbid curiosity, Greg leaned closer and peered in. "Let's get out of here, this place is freaking me out!"

The Key West cemetery.

Photo: Gregory Hummel

The Key West Cemetery was no place to be at night. Though sections of the grounds resembled the traditional style of graveyard with in-ground burials and the standard horseshoe shaped head stones, the majority of the area was shadowed by family crypts, vaults, mausoleums, and what the local kids called "coffin condos," referring to the new section of the cemetery where vaults were built four high and twelve wide stacked on top of one another like a condominium.

Peter and Greg could barely make out the black and white images in the photos affixed to the front of each one as they crept by.

In the daylight the cemetery had a comforting, almost peaceful feeling about it, but as the sun began to set and night rolled in the comfort was overcome by a feeling of mystery, and an eerie aura surrounded the burial grounds. The fact that the cemetery closed at sundown only added to the sense of adventure; not in a criminal way, but more like a feeling that you were not supposed to be there. Maybe it would have been different if they had climbed the gate or broken one of the locks, but none of that was necessary as the chain link portion bordering Angela Street provided plenty of opportunities to walk right in.

Peter had lived in Key West for nearly eight months now. Like many other locals he had developed a fascination of sorts with the graveyard and would often go out of his way to pass through the grounds on his way to work. As the two walked from grave to grave Peter explained to Greg that most of the burials were above ground because of the low elevation of the Keys and the fact that the coral and limestone base was nearly impossible to dig into.

To demonstrate his point, Peter took a lighter from his front pocket and stopped in front of one of the low lying tombs. As the flame illuminated the ground Greg noticed that the marble had suffered years of erosion. Even with the aid of the lighter the name on the stone was impossible to read. In the middle of the grave was a small section where the marble had caved in, and out of pure, morbid curiosity, Greg leaned closer and peered in.

"Let's get out of here, this place is freaking me out!" He looked as if he had seen a ghost, but in reality it was only a leg bone or an arm bone. Peter managed to calm him down and they continued their journey. "Follow me this way," Peter beckoned. "I'll show you where the Key Deer and the dogs are buried." He figured this would calm Greg down. It was probably best to wait until later to show him the tomb that was rumored to be home to a Key West vampire.

After forty-five minutes of exploring it was time for a cigarette break. Peter selected a waist high rectangular tomb as their bench, surrounded by a family-size mausoleum on either side, and a large oak behind. These would help to hide the light of the cigarette from the neighbors surrounding the cemetery who seemed to have nothing better to do than call the police. As they lit up their cigarettes, both let out a sigh of relief as if they were on intermission. With their guard down, neither man heard her approaching, and by the time she was there it was too late to run.

She seemed to appear out of nowhere. She was a large lady who appeared to be of Bahamian descent, dressed in a dark patterned wrap dress, with gold hoop earrings that looked like they belonged on her wrist more than in her ears. Her broad frame dismissed any chance of escape and her eyes seemed to glow an eerie white.

"You boys should have more respect for the dead!" she scolded them. "Get off that tomb and put your cigarette out."

Both Peter and Greg scrambled to comply, apologized profusely and turned to leave. Both were stopped in their tracks.

"Not so fast you two," she ordered with a firm hand on each shoulder. "I've watched you both tromping all over everyone's graves like they were stepping stones in the water and it's time that you learned an important lesson. If I don't teach it to you, maybe one of the other residents in here will."

"The first official settlement of Key West happened around 1890," she began.

Peter and Greg looked at each other in disbelief. Moments before they did not know if they would be leaving the cemetery alive, and here they were getting a history lesson. The story continued.

"One of the early settlers here was a Bahamian immigrant named Robert Albury. Living in a largely undeveloped city, still separate from the mainland, Robert spent most of his days fishing for grunts and diving for conch in the waters surrounding the island. Keep in mind this was no easy job, but it was one that Robert loved. In fact the only thing close to his love of fishing was his love of a lady. Unfortunately it was a love that would prove fatal.

"Christopher Darvel was another Bahamian settler who arrived in Key West shortly after Albury. They say he was a striking man with distinguished features, as well as an accomplished ship builder in the Bahamas. He used his craftsmanship in Key West to help build the houses, and he dreamed of the day when he would build a house for the girl of his dreams, Miss Louisa Thomas.

"Not much is known about Louisa. Her story seems to have been lost over the years, but she was said to be the object of both Christopher Darvel's and Robert Albury's affection."

"Does this have anything to do with the cemetery?" Peter cautiously asked in a feeble attempt to excuse himself. The mysterious woman ignored his question and continued with her story.

"There are some who say Louisa was the daughter of a sea captain, others say a doctor. Every one seems to agree that Louisa was one of the most beautiful women on the island, and was pursued by many of the men here. Darvel and Albury both proposed marriage to her and before long a rivalry developed that would soon turn deadly.

"One summer evening Christopher arrived at Louisa's home to find Robert on the front porch. A verbal argument turned physical an Albury was thrown from the porch hitting his head on a large coral roc in the garden, knocking him unconscious.

"Louisa's family took him in and attempted to help him, but th injury was serious and little could be done. Slipping in and out of con sciousness, Albury looked at his murderer for the last time sayin; 'Some things may go unpunished, but this is not one. Revenge th does not come in life will come in death, and both you and your fam ly will suffer for the injustice you have caused.'

"Robert Albury died later that evening and was one of the first to be buried in this cemetery. His final resting place is in the old section where they were put below ground. His death was deemed accidental and Christopher Darvel was let off. Louisa left the island in despair, sick with grief over a death she felt she had caused.

"Darvel went on to marry another and raised a beautiful family here on the island. He became both a father and a grandfather and had all but forgotten about his enemy's curse until one tragic day after the hurricane of 1909.

"Elizabeth Camp, Darvel's granddaughter was passing through the cemetery with her friend Dean Johnson. It was rumored in town that the two would soon marry. One minute the couple was walking side by side and talking, the next, Elizabeth was no where to be found.

"Johnson frantically searched the cemetery, but finding no holes she may have slipped into, headed into town to continue the search. The next morning there was still no sign of Elizabeth, so a search party was organized and headed up by her grandfather.

"Three days passed before the body was found. It seems that the hurricane had washed away portions of the limestone bedding, weakening one of the tombs and causing it to cave in, sucking Elizabeth into the ground. Rescue people were not able to detect the narrow opening immediately.

"Christopher Darvel was called to the site to identify the body, and was horrified as he peered at the tomb. The past came to life as he looked at the tombstone and saw the name Robert Albury. It seems that his enemy's promise of revenge made so many years ago had come true.

"In a bizarre twist of fate, Darvel and two other members of the search team developed cholera from exposure to the wet grave sites and died in a matter of days.

"So now I will let you go, but you must leave the cemetery at once. When you return make sure you show the proper respect for the dead and stay on the main pathways. Perhaps your ancestors had rivals too, and in Key West, an enemy's tomb is the last place you want to be caught dead."

She silently disappeared without a trace. Greg and Peter stood silent for a moment and then headed for the gate as quickly as they could. Neither one spoke until they returned to Peter's house, and even then conversation was limited to questioning whether or not the night's events had really happened.

Peter still questions it to this day. He continues to visit the cemetery, though not as frequently as before. His visits are now limited to daylight hours, and he is always very careful not to step on anyone's tomb.

Photo: Gregory Hummel

A Promise Kept

When I finished on the phone I started walking to her but she turned the corner out the door. Turning the same corner seconds later, I found an empty backyard. She was gone like that.

The Marrero Guest Mansion is haunted by the friendly spirit of Enriquetta.

Photos: Rob O'Neal

A sharp rap on the door sounded through the Marrero House, evoking a "what now" look on Enriquetta's face. Preparing the house for Francisco's return was more than a handful, and with eight children in the house the last thing she needed was another visitor.

"Would somebody get that please," she called from the top of the stairs; but the knocking continued and after a few moments it became evident who would be answering the door. Enriquetta's face showed her displeasure, and as she hurried down the stairs to the entryway the new crystal chandelier began to shake and sway from the vibration of her heavy footsteps.

As she noticed the swaying for the first time, a brief smile swept across Enriquetta's face, but not because of the expense, by any means. Francisco had more than his fair share of the Key West cigar market with his six hundred employees, so money was not a consideration. But like the other valuable items that made their house a home, it served as an assurance that the children would be taken care of no matter what happened to her or Francisco.

Upon reaching the bottom of the stairs Enriquetta took a moment to fix her hair and put on a proper smile before opening the door. Though the stranger had an awkward expression on his face and kept looking to the ground, Enriquetta was gracious.

"How can I help you?" she asked.

"Are you Enriquetta Marrero?"

Enriquetta nodded her head and looked inquisitively at the man.

"Are you married to Francisco Marrero?"

She nodded her head again.

"I regret to inform you that you husband has passed on."

Enriquetta stared back in disbelief for a moment, then began to cry as the man offered his condolences and explained that the death had taken place in Cuba and was a result of causes unknown.

It seemed like only yesterday that Francisco had kissed her good-bye and promised he would return as soon as he wrapped up a few loose ends for the cigar business. Now he was gone and she was left alone to raise the kids. Little did she know that the worst was yet to come.

In the six months that followed Enriquetta managed to do alright. With her home in the center of the business district she did not have many close friends, but there were the many acquaintances from the cigar industry and most importantly, the children for whom she knew she had to be strong. It was them she credited for helping her through Francisco's death, but then just as things seemed to be getting better, the family was delivered a fatal blow. Francisco had a first wife whom he had never divorced and she was in Key West to claim their home and cigar business as her own.

A bitter court battle followed her arrival and when all was said and done, Maria Ignacia Garcia de Marrero was named administratrix of Francisco's estate. Enriquetta not only lost her home and the cigar company, but all of the house's possessions as well. She was to be left penniless on the streets of Key West with her eight children. The final documents were signed and sealed on June 16th, 1891 a few hours before Enriquetta was to be evicted.

As the eviction grew near, a small crowd gathered in front of the Marrero house. All were silent as the children came through the door for the last time with their mother in the lead. Before reaching the steps leading down from the porch, Enriquetta placed her arms around the shoulders of two of the children, gathering the others close to her side. Though she had avoided looking at the people who gathered just a few feet in front of her until this point, she now looked straight into every eye present and made a final promise.

"You are witnessing a great injustice today," she announced. "And though you are removing me from my home, you should know that this house is rightfully mine; and with God as my witness I will always remain here in spirit."

No one said a word. The crowd stepped back as the family walked down the staircase and off into the streets. In the years that followed all of the Marreros' lives were claimed, many by consumption or diphtheria.

Francisco's first wife eventually sold everything and returned to

Cuba. The house has since served a number of purposes ranging from casino and bordello to restaurant and guest house, with Enriquetta's spirit being reported through all of the years. For the fifteen years prior to 1999, her home was known as the Colours Guest Mansion which hosted countless sightings, stories, and strange ghostly encounters. Many of these occurrences have been recorded, and the pages that follow reflect a ghost log of individual's experiences. In reading them it becomes apparent that Enriquetta's final promise was one she definitely kept and no matter what should become of the house on 410 Fleming Street, it will always be home to Enriquetta.

Ghost Log: Justin, Owner

It has now been three nights that I have stayed in the house and my suspicions of not being alone were confirmed by the next door neighbor. On my first night here I was constantly awakened by a tapping sound, but I could not figure out what it was. When I got up to look around the noise stopped. The next night it happened again and I realized it was the sound of someone typing. It was coming from the next room, but I was alone, and there was no typewriter in the house. The next day while Gerald and I were painting, the radio started changing stations all on its own, and I have noticed electrical devices such as the air conditioners turning themselves on. The strangest thing has to be the lights. Though the power was not turned on until yesterday, lights have been going on and off through out the house. Gerald has noticed this as well. The neighbor said the ghost's name is Henrietta. Let's just hope she is friendly.

Ghost Log: Justin, Owner

Well it seems that she is a friendly ghost, or at least a helpful one. Last night I told Gerald we would have to wake up early for the furniture shipment coming in from Miami. We were both pretty tired from stripping the floors, so we called it an early night.

At about 2:00 a.m. I woke up to three loud knocks on my door, and opening it up I found Gerald asking me what I wanted. He was claiming someone had been knocking on his door. I was too tired to argue so I went back to sleep, only to be awakened again. The banging was so loud this time that it shook the door jamb back and forth. I got out of bed and swung the door open, but the hallway was empty. A second later Gerald opened his door saying the same thing had happened again.

With all of the ghost stuff we were a little bit spooked, so we decided it was in our best interest to stay up and headed downstairs for coffee. After about ten minutes the truck pulled up in front of the house with our furniture shipment...hours earlier than expected. I think the ghost was anxious to have her house renovated and somehow knew that the truck was arriving early. I guess she didn't want us to miss the shipment.

Ghost Log: Michael, Manager

In the years that I have been working here I have had a countless number of encounters with Enriquetta, but the thing I find most interesting is the chandelier in the entryway. Whenever someone is in a bad mood, or even just a nasty person, the chandelier will start to swing back and forth. I get the feeling Enriquetta does not like the bad energy coming into her house.

Most of the time the people check out after only a couple of minutes in the house, and it has become so predictable that I have their paperwork all ready for them when they come down. The ones who stay though are usually in for some big trouble.

Last week some grumpy people checked in and the chandelier started. I kept waiting but they never came down. The next two days they had nothing but problems. Four keys broke off in their door, the air conditioner stopped working, light bulbs in their room were constantly blowing out and the bath tub flooded. It is not very easy explaining to a guest that the ghost does not like them, that is for sure.

Ghost Log: Joel, Guest

Dear Colours, (former name of Marrero House)

I came to your hotel last week knowing nothing about it being haunted, but in no time had an encounter that I thought you might like to hear. My friend Kieran and I had been sleeping for about two hours when I awoke to the feeling that someone else was in the room.

Looking around I noticed a transparent woman standing at the foot of the bed, and believe it or not she was brushing her hair in the mirror.

My first thought was that I must wake Kieran, but before I could do a thing the lady turned to me and raised a finger to her lips motioning me to be quiet. I know this all sounds crazy, so I paid no attention to her and tried to wake him anyway. Next thing I knew she appeared by the side of my bed, put her hand out and covered my mouth to stop me from saying anything. This freaked me out so much that I pushed up right through her and it was then that she disappeared. I talked to one of your employees there and he told me it is a friendly ghost. Just thought you would want to know.

Ghost Log: Evan & Ryan, Guests

We had been staying here for two days knowing nothing about a ghost until one morning at breakfast some other guests spoke of their experience. Evan laughed at the idea saying that if there was really a ghost in the house she would have given us a sign.

We went out to Duval Street for dinner and returned at about 10:00 p.m. to find that our room reeked of lavender perfume. Figuring someone was playing a joke on us we aired the room out, and asked the managers if they had let anyone into our room. Not only did they say no, but they had been in the lobby all night and we were the only guests on the second floor. No one had been upstairs.

Still a bit suspicious, we went to sleep joking about the ghost again. At 3:00 a.m. we were both startled awake by the same sweet smell. She has certainly made a believer out of me.

Ghost Log: Abraham, Employee

I am convinced she doesn't like me. O.K. so I have never seen her, but she is the easiest one to blame when something goes wrong.

Last week, for example, it was a busy day at the pool and we ran out of towels. I rushed to get a load through the laundry, and when they were finished I was walking alongside the pool to distribute them when someone asked me why we had run out. "It's Enriquetta's fault," I told them, and the next thing I knew I was in the pool with the stack of towels. People who saw this happen swear that it looked like I was pushed, and I can't help but think Enriquetta did not like being blamed. This is not the first time something like this has happened.

Ghost Log: Lee, Manager

Two days after expressing my doubts about this house being haunted I had a very strange encounter. While taking a reservation on the telephone my attention was diverted to a lady standing in the front doorway. I knew she was not a guest at the house, so I found it strange that she had been able to enter without a key, and on top of that she was dressed in a style that you don't often see in Key West in this day and age.

When she realized I had seen her, she started walking towards me. Just as she passed I was given a smile and a nod, then she waited by the back exit as if she had a question. When I finished on the phone I started walking to her but she turned the corner out the door. Turning the same corner seconds later I found an empty back yard. She was gone like that.

I have since gone through every possibility in my head but have been unable to explain her sudden disappearance. I now welcome stories from others. They might have experiences, but I saw her.

Ghost Log: Kristin & Eileene, Guests

I woke up at 3:00 a.m. on the dot. My arm had a tingling sensation as if it had fallen asleep, but as I looked to the side I saw a torso dressed in white, a flowing gown sitting on my arm. No head, no arms, just a torso.

When I realized I was not dreaming, I went to wake Eileene, and as she she started to stir the figure rose up off my arm and went to the far right corner of our room where she stayed for a few minutes. As Eileene began trying to communicate with her she went diagonally across the room and into the bathroom. When we checked the bathroom, no one was there. Hopefully I can change my flight and stay another night. I think if I do I will see her again.

Psychic Report:

While on the ghost tour I saw Enriquetta standing on the porch listening to Stacey tell the story. Enriquetta still sees the house as it was. I saw shadows about her as well which my guides identified as her children who are tied to their mother–not the property. I asked Enriquetta if she would like to go to the light and she declined preferring to stay with her home for now. She is fond of Stacey and appreciated the sympathy she conveys when telling the story. Enriquetta can be seen by any guest who is clairvoyant or sensitive. I suspect she is seen a lot because there are a lot of us out there and Enriquetta scans each guest for the potential to communicate.

Author's Note: Rick Jenkins and Buddy Dyess purchased Marrero's Guest Mansion and made some incredible changes. In addition to the fine antiques and incredible attention to detail throughout their new home, they changed the name of the house from Colours to Marrero's in honor of the friendly spirits they share the guest mansion with. Whether you live in Key West or are visiting for pleasure, you owe it to yourself to spend at least one night in this fine guest house. Thank you Buddy and Rick for all that you have done. Enriquetta must be very proud.

A Promise Kept

Top photo: *Francisco Marrero.*

Bottom Photo: *Francisco & Enriquetta's marriage license.*

Pages 98 & 99: Documents showing transfer of estate from Francisco to Enriquetta, to Francisco's first wife.

Documents & Photos: courtesy of the Marrero Guest Mansion and Rob O'Neal

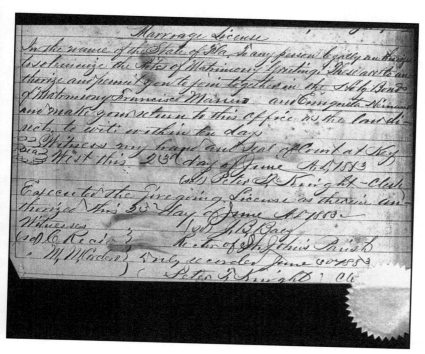

For Better or For Worse

When the time came, Carl knew what he must do. By the light of the moon he slipped into the graveyard and removed her body from its tomb. Transporting her in his wingless airplane, von Cosel took the body home and began the process.

Eleyna Hoyos.

Photo: courtesy of Monroe County Library

Count Carl von Cosel.

Photo: courtesy of Monroe County Library

Eleyna Hoyos was as beautiful as they came. Raised in a well- to-do Cuban family that had fallen on hard times in Key West, Eleyna had raven black ringlets of hair and was described as full of life by all who knew her. Charming and graceful, she seemed to have it all, including a handsome young husband named Luis Mesa. The newlyweds had a promising future together and were preparing for their first child when things took a turn for the worse.

Young Eleyna had a miscarriage, and shortly after she became ill and was diagnosed with tuberculosis, a contagious and incurable disease at the time. Her husband left her, and due to her parents' misfortune, they would be unable to provide Eleyna with the care she needed. Enter the picture Count Carl von Cosel.

Count von Cosel was a self-proclaimed Count, as well as many other things. A German citizen, his real name was Carl Tanzler, and though he was well-read in many subjects, it is doubt-ful that he had any real schooling in the various fields he practiced. One of these fields was medicine, and it was his work with x-rays that got him a job at the Marine Hospital and led to his first chance encounter with Eleyna.

In his memoirs, the Count often talked of his search for a bride. Though he already had a wife and a two children in Zephyrhills, Florida, he realized he had only settled, so he left them to search for his soul-mate. He would know her when he found her, for she had visited him before.

When Eleyna walked into the Marine hospital, Count von Cosel's thoughts flashed back to Germany thirty years prior. Though it would still be 10 years before her birth, an apparition of Eleyna appeared to Carl with the Ghost of the Countess Anna who was one of Von Cosel's ancestors. The Countess told him of his des-tiny and as the veil was lifted on the mysterious apparition, he saw the face of Eleyna, his bride to be.

Realizing he had finally met his future bride, the Count was quite nervous in taking her blood sample. He was even more excit-ed, and it is said that he fell in love with Eleyna, when he x-rayed her chest. This excitement soon turned to sorrow. The diagnosis was bad. The tuberculosis had advanced and death was certain, but von Cosel would not give up hope on his new found love quite so easily.

He visited her every day and provided radiation treatments free of charge. He showered her with gifts and expressed his desire to marry her, but Eleyna always declined saying she was ill, and perhaps they would marry when she recovered. She never did.

Eleyna died just days before Halloween and was buried in a simple tomb. The Count could not bear to see her precious body rot in the ground, so, with her father's permission, he had the body exhumed and properly embalmed, then placed in a special coffin and crypt, equipped complete with a telephone so he could speak to his deceased love. He visited her everyday, and believing he could communicate with her spirit, the two devised a plan to reunite Eleyna's body and soul.

When the time came, Carl knew what he must do. By the light of the moon he slipped into the graveyard and removed her body from its' tomb. Transporting her in his wingless airplane, von Cosel took the body home and began the process. According to his memoirs, Eleyna's spirit now began to speak to him, providing instructions on the recreation of her body.

The funeral home had really botched the job of embalming. When Carl opened her inner coffin, he found Eleyna's body in an advanced state of decomposition and most of her skin was torn off as it stuck to the now fallen lining.

The process of rebuilding Eleyna's body was difficult, but the Count was able to reconstruct her face magnificently with mortician's wax and plaster. Her head was completed with two glass eyeballs and locks of her own hair. People who later saw her said the face was an incredible likeness.

The body, however, presented a problem. When her corpse was removed from the coffin it weighed a mere 40 pounds. Von Cosel had to bring the weight to at least 100 pounds, and he did so by stuffing her body with rags and saturating her in a custom made tank filled with embalming fluids and antiseptics. Eleyna's decaying skin was replaced with silk, as this was the only material as smooth to the touch as her own skin had been. This was very important to the Count as we would later discover.

For seven years Eleyna shared a bed with the Count in a small, out-of-the-way shack on Flagler Avenue. Rumors began to circulate around town about the strange happenings in the Count's house, and eventually reached Eleyna's sister Nana. Nana went to investigate, and upon peering through the Count's window, she stood in disbelief.

Count Carl von Cosel sat in the small room playing a melody on the organ. In the bed next to him was a fully reconstructed Eleyna, wearing a wedding dress with a ring on her finger. Her sister had been dead for nine years.

Police arrested von Cosel for wanton and willful destruction of a tomb. Eleyna's body was placed on display in the local funeral chapel where over 6,800 people came to see the body. Key West became a media circus and the story spread around the world.

The case never went to trial. A heart broken Count von Cosel returned to Zephyrhills, living just miles from his first wife. He spent his remaining days writing his memoirs. Hours after the count had fled Key West, a mysterious explosion blew up the crypt he had crafted for Eleyna which now stood vacant.

Because of all of the media hype, as well as the Count's obsession, Eleyna's body was cut into small pieces and placed in an 18 inch long box. She was buried at midnight in a secret location. Some people say she is in the cemetery, others under the oldest house, but no one will ever be sure. All three men involved in her burial have since taken that secret to their graves.

Count Von Cosel eventually died as well. After his death, doctors who had examined Eleyna's body released some disturbing news. Count Von Cosel had consummated his marriage to Eleyna.

As an appropriate ending to the story of a love that would not die; when Carl's body was found he was lying on top of an open coffin, holding in his arms a replica of Eleyna de Hoyos.

The search for Eleyna's ghost continues, and though stories arise from time to time claiming to know where her presence is, none have been verified. None the less, the spirit of Eleyna will always live on in Key West.

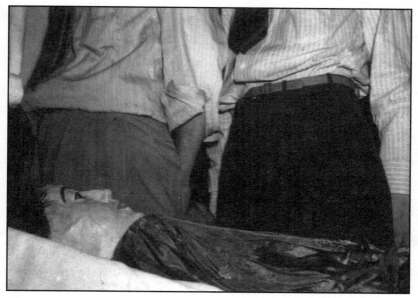

The body of Eleyna de Hoyos on display at the funeral home.
Photo: courtesy of the Monroe Public Library

In Closing

Ghosts have been good to me. From the moment I entered the corporate business world I was looking for a way to get out of it and through a series of events too strange to be coincidences, I ended up in Key West.

My first exposure to ghosts came from Mrs. Ubercedar, my kindergarten teacher. Not only did she amuse the class with tales of her ghost, but she had an actual photograph of it. I was amazed.

My interest continued with varying degrees until my mid-twenties when I took a flight to England to visit the woman who I am now proud to call my wife. Looking for something to read on the flight I picked up a book on ghosts from the airport newsstand and immediately my interest was rejuvenated.

We traveled from England to Scotland, and while looking for a book store in Edinburgh, Cindy and I happened across a ghost tour sign. My eyes lit up and Cindy's rolled. It was well below freezing and the last thing she wanted to do was walk around in the cold for an hour, so we made the obvious compromise. I left her in the pub and went on the tour by myself, and by the end of that evening I knew what I wanted to do in life. Upon returning to the United States I quit my job and headed to the most haunted city in the United States to start a Ghost Tour.

Arriving in Charleston, South Carolina I was full of vigor and eager to start my new career. After conducting some preliminary research I went for a walk around town to try and get a feel for the place, but my world came crashing down as I discovered that Charleston already had a ghost tour.

Having been around long enough to know that you do not move in on someone else's ghosts, I headed to Fort Lauderdale to spend Easter with my parents, wondering what in the heck I was going to do with my life now that I had quit my job and my ghost town had fallen through. I looked for other towns, but none seemed right, and just when

In Closing

I was considering going back to the hotel business, a friend from the past called my parents house looking for me.

As it turned out, Greg was working in a hotel in Key West. I told him my idea and he suggested moving to the second oldest city in Florida. I had nothing to lose, so I packed up and headed South.

My first week of research turned up nothing, and after two weeks I was ready to call it quits and head home when another strange thing happened. A voice from somewhere told me to go back to the library, and though I had already been five times in as many days, I decided to give it one last chance. On this day I met Tom Hambright who approached me in the Florida History section and asked if he could help me find anything.

"I'm looking for a book on ghosts of Key West," I told him.

"There are none," was his response.

"No books or no ghosts?" I asked, expecting the worst. Luckily he meant books, and walking back into the library vault, Tom emerged a moment later with an inch thick file full of newspaper clippings on ghosts and voodoo. I plotted the houses on a map and set off to do some research, and two years later, here I am.

The ghosts still have an effect on me, and the stories keep coming in. If you enjoyed reading this book, I invite you to join us on the tour for updated stories and additional haunted locations. To better help you in locating your favorite haunted places, I have included a haunted directory in the pages that follow. Most of the places are haunted, or related in some way to the supernatural, so when you visit, be sure to tell them where you heard about them.

Until next time, happy haunting.

The Haunted Directory

The Artist House
Bed & Breakfast
534 Eaton Street
Key West, FL 33040
(305) 296-3977

Audubon House & Gardens
Museum & Garden Tour
205 Whitehead Street
Key West, FL 33040
(305) 294-2116

Captain Tony's Saloon
Bar/Saloon
428 Greene Street
Key West, FL 33040
(305) 294-1838

Curry Mansion Inn
Guest Mansion/House Tour
511 Caroline Street
Key West, FL 33040
(305) 294-5349

Cypress House
Guest House
601 Caroline Street
Key West, FL 33040
(305) 294-6969

East Martello Museum
Museum/Robert the Doll
3501 South Roosevelt Blvd.
Key West, FL 33040
(305) 296-3913

The Eaton Lodge
Bed & Breakfast
511 Eaton Street
Key West, FL 33040
(305) 292-2170

Fort Zachary Taylor
Historic Fort and Beaches
(305) 292-6713

Ghost Tours of Key West
Haunted Walks
P.O. Box 4766
Key West, FL 33041
(305) 294-9255

Hard Rock Cafe
Food, Drinks, Souvenirs
313 Duval Street
Key West, FL 33040
(305) 293-0230

Harrison Gallery & Music
Undying Love Book & Tapes
825 White Street
Key West, FL 33040
(305) 294-0609

Hemingway House
Museum/Tour
907 Whitehead Street
Key West, FL 33040
(305) 294-1575

Heritage House Museum
House Tour/Pirate's Well
410 Caroline Street
Key West, FL 33040

Holiday Inn La Concha
Hotel
430 Duval Street
Key West, FL 33040
(305) 296-2991

The Little White House
Museum/Tour
111 Front Street
Key West, FL 33040
(305) 294-9911

Marrero's Guest Mansion
Guest House
410 Fleming Street
Key West, FL 33040
(305) 294-6977

The Red Rooster Inn
Hotel
709 Truman Avenue
Key West, FL 33040
(305) 296-6558

Ripley's Believe It or Not
Odditorium
527 Duval Street
Key West, FL 33040
(305) 293-9686

Saint Paul's Episcopal Church
Cathedral
401 Duval Street
Key West, FL 33040
(305) 296-5142

Theatre de Seance
Victorian Era Seances
429 Caroline Street
Key West, FL 33040
(305) 292-2040

The Wrecker's Museum
Oldest House Tour
322 Duval Street
Key West, FL 33040
(305) 294-9502

About the Author

David Sloan was born in Wayne, Pennsylvania and grew up in Richardson, Texas. After graduating Florida International University, David served as General Manager with a Florida cruise line for three years before trading in his Bachelor of Science degree for a lantern and top hat.

David is currently President of the Key West Tour Association, Inc. and lives in Key West with his wife Cindy, and their two cats Vladimir and Dr. Jeckyl.

E-mail David directly at keysghoul@aol.com

To Order Additional Copies
Of This Book

1) Send a check or money order to:
KeyWest Tour Association
P.O. Box 4766
Key West, FL 33041

2) Fax your address and credit card billing information to:
Key West Tour Association
(305) 294-5175

3) Visit us online:
www.hauntedtours.com

4) Call Ghost Tours direct:
(305) 294-9255

Wholesale prices are available for purchases of 12 copies or more. Personalized, autographed copies are always available from the author.

If you are in Key West, be sure not to miss The Ghost Tour. Researched and created by *Ghosts of Key West* Author, David Sloan. The Ghost Tour takes you through the shadowy streets aof historic Old Town Key West where ghosts, ghouls and legends come to life. Tours depart nightly year round. For more information call 305-294-9255 or visit us online at: www.hauntedtours.com

Sign Up For Our Newsletter

Keep up to date on all of the latest Key West hauntings with our internet newsletter. Simply send us yoru e-mail address and once a month we will update you on the haunted happenings in town. The newsletter is available free of course. No strings attached. To sign up, send your e-mail to keysghoul@aol.com subject: newsletter

HAPPY HAUNTINGS!